Conquering Anorexia

the route to recovery

Clare Lindsay

SUMMERSDALE

Summersdale Publishers Ltd
46 West Street
Chichester
West Sussex
PO19 1RP
United Kingdom

www.summersdale.com

Printed and bound in Great Britain by Creative Print & Design, Wales.

ISBN 1 84024 096 2

To Roger, with love

For loving me and loving me and loving me

Acknowledgments

To **Roger Povey, Caryn Waller** and **Chris Hardwick**.
For taking care of me when you didn't have to and for always being there when I needed you.

To all my **sixth form friends**, for being the safety net I didn't need when any of you were around. Thank you.

To **Nick Winney**, for being my friend, and for caring then and now.

To **Ravi Mohan, Scott Lamond, Chris Ward, Andrew Gill** and **Howard Cliff**. Thanks for being great friends and for the fun, the laughter, the caring, and the webbishness that always wrapped round.

To **Dr Markham**, for your kindness and your patience, and for helping me as much as you did.

To **The People who Scare the Workmen**, for seeing in me what I couldn't see myself and for making so much out of so little.

To **Clare Ward**, for opening my mind to a whole new way of living. Thank you for everything.

To **Katie and the staff at St. Andrew's**, for helping me see that the impossible could happen. This book says it all. I can't thank you enough...

To my **college friends at York,** for your support and encouragement, and for making me feel that being mad was quite normal.

To **Caroline, Ci, Gail, Janet, Mary, Nikki** and **Rachel**, for being friends I could always rely on.

To **Dan**, for answering questions I needed answering. Your honesty made things happen.

To **Helen & Giles Nelson, Julia Roberts, Kevin Blair, Simon Turner, Christine Biss, Anthony & Mary Nield** and **Colin Fraser,** for welcoming me to Dundee and for giving Roger and I some of our happiest times.

To **Eileen Howard**, for believing in me and for giving me the opportunity of a lifetime.

To **Collette Brooks, Louise George,** and **everyone I worked with at The Hope Unit**, for all that I learnt during my time spent with you.

To **Simon Potts** for the yellowest of summers and the many wacky times since...

To **Tim Elder** for always boosting my confidence, and **Tony Smith** for believing that this book would happen.

To **Elizabeth Kershaw**, my editor, and **everyone at Summersdale**, for making it happen.

To **John Alcock**, for your kind help.

To **New Order** and to **U2**, for both agreeing to let me use your lyrics.

To **Bob Geldof**, for kindly allowing me to reproduce part of a day that changed everything.

And to **Marcia**, who I'll never forget.

Special Thanks

To **Caryn Waller**, for being a better friend than anyone could hope for. Thank you for everything.

To **Chris Hardwick**, for being a big brother to me and for making me feel protected - always.

To **Colin Fraser**, for the spaghetti that wouldn't fit in the pan... and for being a brilliant friend who always leaves me happy.

To my **Mum & Dad** and **Gary**, for giving me everything I'm most proud of and for putting up with far more than anyone should.

To **Julie & Alan Povey, Joanne, Rob, Jack & Emily**, for always understanding, and for supporting Roger and I in everything we do.

And of course, to **Roger**. The kindest and most loving person I know, my partner, my friend, my everything. Thanks for getting me through this, for always taking the very best care of me and for making the years with you the happiest I've known. But most of all, thank you for loving me. I couldn't have made it without you.

Permission Acknowledgements

I wish to acknowledge and thank the following sources for kindly allowing me to reprint their material.

Lyrics from 'October', U2:
Written by Adam Clayton/David Evans/Paul Hewson/Laurence Mullen 1981 Blue Mountain Music Ltd (for the UK) International Copyright Secured.

Lyrics from 'True Faith', New Order:
Words and Music by Steven Morris, Peter Hook, Bernard Sumner, Gillian Gilbert & Stephen Hague.
Copyright ©_1987 Be Music, administered by Warner Chappell Music Limited, 129 Park Street, London W1 (75%) / Cut Music, administered by MCA Music Limited, 77 Fulham Palace Road, London W6 (25%). Used by permission of Music Sales Limited.
All Rights Reserved. International Copyright Secured.

Definition of Assertiveness:
Stephanie Holland and Clare Ward, *Assertiveness: A Practical Approach*, Winslow Press, 1990.

July 13th 1985, Live-Aid:
Bob Geldof.

Lyrics from 'New Years Day', U2:
Written by Adam Clayton/David Evans/Paul Hewson/Laurence Mullen Copyright ©_1982 Blue Mountain Music Ltd (for the UK) / Mother Music (for the Republic of Ireland) / Taiyo Music Inc (for Japan) / Polygram International Music Publishing Ltd (for the rest of the world).

'Rights Charter':
Stephanie Holland and Clare Ward, *Assertiveness: A Practical Approach*, Winslow Press, 1990.

Diagnostic criteria for clinical definitions of anorexia nervosa, bulimia nervosa and eating disorders not otherwise specified: American Psychiatric Association: Diagnostic and Statistical Manual of Mental Disorders, Fourth Edition. Washington, DC, American Psychiatric Association, 1994.

Contents

St. Andrew's Day Hospital: Day to day progress of the realisations, learning, and development of skills that enabled me to recover completely from both my anorexia and depression.

PART FOUR

Preface

Within the UK at any point in time, up to 200,000 young people will be suffering from anorexia nervosa. Of these young people, most will be in their teens or early twenties, many will have become chronically ill and some will be as young as six years old. Destroying health, happiness and hope, for as many as one in five of these young people, anorexia will prove fatal.

Claiming more lives than any other psychiatric disorder, in this country alone hundreds (possibly thousands) of young people die from anorexia every year. Yet none of these young people need die. In Britain, anorexia need not be a fatal illness. We have the knowledge, the understanding and the professional skills necessary to treat this disorder. And it can be successfully treated – I know it can. I also know that complete recovery from anorexia is perfectly possible – and that it's possible here, in this country.

Why then, if anorexia really can be fully defeated and need not be fatal, should it be that this disorder continues to take so many lives? The answer to this question, I believe, is a simple one. The main reason why up to 20 per cent of anorectics die, is that they believe absolutely that recovery is just not possible. Creating hopelessness, despair and self-defeat, the main reason why anorectics believe that they will never recover, quite simply, is that there has never been any literature available – anywhere – to convince them otherwise.

In order to recover from their illness, anorectics need believable evidence and proof demonstrating that recovery from anorexia is possible. They also need realistic hope based upon explanations and expectations. Written specifically for the anorectic desperate to recover from anorexia, this book aims to provide just this evidence, proof and hope that, up until now, anorectics have been denied.

This book is not simply a theoretical account. Instead, it offers a step-by-step explanation of real recovery from anorexia, and for the first time ever documents and fully explains exactly how this can be achieved. In so doing it provides – at long last – the 'recovery-based' insights and knowledge, explanations and answers, that all anorectics seek but have never before been able to find.

Although the experiences and explanations described throughout this book are based upon recovery from anorexia, the information provided will be of equal relevance to those wishing to recover from bulimia.

Introduction

Anyone who has ever encountered anorexia nervosa, whether in themselves or another, will know only too well the devastating effects of an illness which rapidly grows to control and dominate the lives of those who vulnerably fall into its clutches. Frustrating and difficult to understand, for victim and observer alike anorexia breeds despair and generates hopelessness. Destroying health and happiness, and replacing opportunities with fear and failed attempts at recovery, for both the person trapped within the illness and those who try to help, there can be few things more frightening than believing that anorexia cannot be defeated.

I developed anorexia in 1982, when I was thirteen years old. By the time I had reached my twenties, my anorexia had completely taken over my life and had become a chronic condition from which nobody expected me to recover. Desperately wanting to be well again, throughout the whole time that I was ill I tried as hard as anybody probably could to overcome my difficulties, and yet still I remained stuck. Concerned only with finding information that might help me recover, for more than seven years I hunted out, read and methodically studied everything to do with eating disorders that I could lay my hands upon. I dug out journals, contacted researchers, followed studies and scoured medical book shops up and down the land. As a result, I probably became more knowledgeable about eating disorders than anything else in my life, and yet I still didn't have the answers that I needed in order to overcome my anorexia.

Yes, I gained valuable insight into both anorexia and bulimia, and yes, I reached a point of understanding pretty much everything to do with both disorders themselves; but when it came to finding information explaining *recovery* from anorexia, as hard as I tried, I couldn't find anything written anywhere which was of any real use to me. Convinced at first that I simply hadn't been searching thoroughly enough, when I failed time and time again to find anything in the literature that even attempted to offer me the knowledge that I needed, I could only conclude that recovery from anorexia was impossible.

Scared stupid that I'd never be happy or well again, what I didn't know then was that actually there were only three things crucial to recovery, that I needed but hadn't been able to find. Reflecting almost uncannily all that was missing from the literature, in order to recover fully from my anorexia:

I needed *believable evidence* to prove to me that beating anorexia was possible;
I needed *proof* that it would be possible to find the help that I needed *in this country*; and
I needed a believable *step-by-step explanation of recovery*, to inform me of the exact insight, knowledge, learning, skills, and understanding that I'd need to acquire in order to make my recovery happen.

Unable to find any books documenting any of these essential requirements anywhere, by 1990 I'd given up even hoping that I'd ever beat my anorexia. Spiralling lower and lower as each day passed, when I reached the point of not bothering to even try and cope anymore, I found myself faced with no real option other than to go into full-time therapy. Totally convinced that I wouldn't gain anything from attending this or any other form of therapy, within less than a week of entering the day hospital offered to me, I could sense that somehow I was beginning to make progress.

Terrified that I might lose the knowledge and skills that I'd finally started to gain, in an attempt to hang on to everything of possible use to me, I began to jot down exactly what I perceived to be taking place within and around me. Recording progress and setbacks alike, when I could sense for the first time that I was beginning to find the answers that I needed, I began to document every step of my recovery in a detailed diary that I kept every day.

Providing me with a perfect opportunity to selfishly reflect upon me, me, me, initially I recorded everything purely for my own benefit. Entirely wrapped up in my life, my thoughts and my difficulties, it wasn't until I noticed that my needs, experiences and reactions to therapy, were similar (and sometimes spookily identical) to those in therapy with me, that I began to wonder whether my observations might be of use to other people desperately wanting to overcome anorexia or bulimia.

With the odd feeling that I might be in a position to try and provide others with the believable evidence and proof that would have been so helpful for me, I began to turn my diary into this book. In so doing I have tried to pull together every piece of essential information that anorectics, their families and health care professionals, need but have not had access to until now.

In order to make this information of wide-ranging use to eating disordered people experiencing all sorts of difficulties, most of the learning contained in this book reflects not only my own experiences of anorexia and recovery, but also the experiences of the twenty or so clients in therapy with me. Wherever possible I have tried to capture difficulties and fears, issues and reactions, feelings and behavioural characteristics, common to each of us. I have tried to highlight the crucial realisations, important pieces of learning and the essential life skills that we all needed to develop, and I have attempted to outline those set-backs and significant bits of progress that we often uncannily encountered together.

Beginning at the beginning, in the first part of this book I explore the roots of my difficulties and uncover the personal characteristics and behaviours that I now believe influenced the development of my anorexia. Outlining the thoughts, fears and sensitivities that ruled my life as a child, I describe the worried thinking behind my low self-esteem and I begin to highlight the crucial role that a sense of personal ineffectiveness plays in the development of eating disorders.

Moving on, in the second section of this book I record my experiences of, and reactions to, the varying approaches of therapy that I encountered before attending full-time therapy. I describe the support I received from my GP, document the progress (or lack of it) that I made whilst seeing a psychiatrist and I reflect upon the extremely helpful insight, knowledge and understanding I gained through counselling. When it becomes apparent that my needs require more therapy than counselling alone can provide, I end this section convinced that nothing can help me.

Having finally agreed to attend full-time therapy, in the main body of this book I record my thoughts, feelings and fears, in diary form on a daily basis. Starting from a point of informed but complete personal ineffectiveness, I document precisely *how* I learnt to recover from my anorexia by learning how to think and behave more effectively. Providing insight and answers that no book has ever explained before, in this part of the book I address more than forty issues that my fellow clients and I each needed to tackle, and I explain precisely how I learned to develop the fifteen or so assertive life skills we each needed to master in order to overcome our difficulties. Reflecting upon this learning, I highlight and explain the role that developing assertiveness plays in securing recovery from eating disorders.

Taking forward all of the learning that I have been lucky enough to have had invested in me, in the last section of this book, I concentrate upon knowledge, skills and pieces of learning which I feel to be of greatest potential relevance to others wishing to recover from eating disorders. I describe in detail the benefits to be gained from developing personal assertiveness and I touch upon the possibility that increasing assertiveness might hold the key to the prevention of eating disorders. Finally, I highlight the strategies I used to tackle necessary issues and difficulties, and I outline helpful ways of thinking. Providing a foundation from which personal effectiveness can be developed, I also include a number of self-help strategies and self-awareness exercises.

PART ONE

Living with Anorexia

Thirty-four minutes past six. I've just woken up and wish I hadn't. Fantastic, I feel fat. Another day of thinking about food and thinking about food and nothing else. Another stinking day. Let me get back to sleep. Can't. I can't stop thinking about food. I can't get the raisin jar out of my mind. I want one, just one. Yes just one to settle my mind and let me sleep again. No I can't. If I have one I'll want another and another and I won't be able to stop and I'll eat and eat and eat and I'll end up even fatter and I won't be able to eat for the next week and I might not be able to help myself and I won't be able to cope and... Oh God I'm hungry. Why did I have to wake up? Why do I have to be able to think? I wish I couldn't think. How am I going to get through today? I wonder how much I weigh this morning, last night I was disgusting – HUGE. Am I still the same size? Can't cope if I am. Panic. I can't see how big I am. What if I'm even bigger than last night? Can't be, that couldn't be possible. Nobody could be bigger than I was last night – no one. But what if I am? What if I have piled on tonnes of pounds more? What am I going to do? I'm never going to lose this. Hell. I feel awful. My legs, my stomach, everything – ME. They're all disgusting. Can't bring myself to look at them. Offensive. That's all I am. I hate it, I hate being me. I daren't stand on the scales. I'll weigh too much and I won't be able to stand it. Why can't I be thin? What have I done to deserve this? I wonder if I've put on weight overnight. Maybe I've lost a bit. No I can't have done, I feel bigger now than I did yesterday. Am I? Why can't I tell? I need to know. God I need to know but I daren't stand on the scales. Why can't I just lose weight? If I could get down to five and a half, no five stone, I'd be happy. I know I would. I'd feel better than I do now as I am – FAT. What do I look like? Don't want to know. I feel all swollen. Swollen and huge and fat. Repulsive. Look at me, I'm awful. Can't get out of bed, I can't be seen like this – I'm horrible. Horrible and everyone will hate me. I can't stand this, just look at me, my face is fat and everything. Why can't I be thin, I'm never going to be thin enough, I might as well give in. What's the point? I don't want there to be a point anymore. I wish I was still asleep. Six thirty-nine. Hell it's not even seven yet and I'm fed up with today already. Raisins, bloody raisins. Why can't I get food out of my mind? Raisins, muesli, Brazil nuts, dates, toast, kitkats. Kitkats, I could murder one. No. I'm not going to have any of them. I know I can't so I might as well forget about them. Think of something else. What am I going to do today? I don't want to do anything today. I'm too fat. I can't even be bothered to get out of bed – don't want to anyway. I just want to sleep. I shouldn't but I do. Ahhhhh… What's the point? Piss off world. Just piss off and leave me alone. Alone and asleep. Blue skies again, bloody sodding perfect blue, another sunny day. Why? I don't want it to be sunny, I can't be bothered with it anymore. It makes everything worse. All it does is signify everything that everyone else enjoys and makes me feel guilty. Guilty for not doing what I should do, guilty for not wanting to be here anymore and guilty for feeling depressed when I've got no reason and don't know why. I feel bad enough as it is. I know I should be making the most of the summer. I know I should be up enjoying myself and having fun like everyone else. I know I'm wasting time and fun and enjoyment and everything I should be living for, but I can't help it. I just can't. I don't enjoy anything anymore and I hate it. I WISH IT WOULD RAIN. Maybe if it rained I wouldn't feel so bad, maybe tomorrow. Hell I'm hungry. I'll have another can of Diet Coke. I've even got to keep these secret now. Don't want mam and dad to know how much of this stuff I'm drinking. I hope someone's eaten the bread and butter pudding left in the fridge last night. If it's still there it'll drive me mad. I want to eat it but I know I can't. I ate too much yesterday, I'm too fat, I don't deserve to eat and I'll hate myself. I should be able to control myself like everyone else. Kitkats, I want some kitkat and there's one in the fridge. No, it'll make me fat and I'll regret it. Anyway if I eat something now I'll want to eat all day. Why can't I get back to sleep… wish today was over. Why can't it be? Eighteen hours to go before bed again. Hell. Fat, guilty and hungry – why can't I just sleep all the time, why do I have to be conscious? Who designed life to incorporate waking up? They shouldn't have bothered, life creates nothing but misery and I don't see any point to it. Is this normal? Are my thoughts normal? Does everyone feel so bad about life or am I the only one? Is it just me? Do other people ever actually WANT to get up? But is that normal, can it possibly be? I think I'm going mad. Why can't I get up, why can't I enjoy myself – why can't I be normal? I should be able to be like everyone else, it can't be that difficult. I shouldn't want to not get up, I should... Sod it, nobody knows what it's like being me. I'm too fat to keep thoughts of food from my mind and it's driving me crazy. Why do I feel so guilty, why don't I understand what the hell's happening to me? What is happening to me? Shit I'm running out of Diet Coke, I'll have to get up to buy some more. I don't want to get up, I really don't want to. Waste of space, useless, pathetic, crap – what am I doing here? Nothing makes sense any more and I don't know anything other than that I wish I could just switch off. Why won't my mind give up and give me a break? I'm fed up, I want a release and I can't stand this. Seven twenty-one, nearly half past. Six and a half hours to go and then I'll have something to eat. I'll have half an apple and a finger of kitkat. No, I'll save the kitkat ' till later, I'll have a coffee with the apple instead. Two o'clock, what can I do until then? Why's my life so bloody awful? Why can't I eat without putting on weight? I'm sick of feeling fat and I'm sick of wishing every day away. It wouldn't be so bad if I didn't have to experience the wanting between meals and if I didn't feel all the time that I should be having fun. This is getting me nowhere, I'm still going to have to get up and I still don't want to. Another day thinking about food, another day fighting thoughts – I wish they'd leave me alone. Dread – that's all I've got to look forward to. Dread dread dread. I want that kitkat, just a tiny bit, a tiny bit off the corner, just enough to taste the chocolate. A tiny bit won't hurt me and it'll help settle my mind. I won't want any more if I just get a taste of it. Less than ten calories worth, there's nothing wrong with that. A tiny corner. Yes and then I won't be hungry anymore and I'll easily be able to wait until two. Maybe... should I have a date as well? Another fifteen calories, that's not the end of the world. Twenty-five in total and I'm going to be next to the date cupboard anyway when I get the kitkat. And I'll make myself a coffee to warm my mouth and enhance the sweetness. Yeah, that's what I'll do. What time is it? Twenty-three to eight. Damn it, it's not even eight yet. If I eat something now there's no way I'll last until two without eating again. No way. I'll have to wait. If I eat now it'll be fatal. I won't be able to stop myself, I'll lose control of everything, I'll just stuff myself and stuff myself and I'll get fatter and fatter and I'll hate myself even more than I do now. I can't. I can't let myself do it, I'll have to wait. Why am I so useless? Food, food, food – I hate it. Wish I could just throw it all out. Why can't I forget about it and get on with my life without it? Why does it have to make things so impossible for me? I wish it'd never been invented – stupid idea. Twenty to eight, seventeen hours at least to go until I'm out of it again. I hope I don't dream tonight. Round and round in bloody circles. God I wish it would rain.

The first feeling I had on waking each morning was that of being fat. My first thoughts would always be of food, followed immediately by despair on realising that a) I was awake, and that b) I was still too fat to eat. Scaring all life from me, for as long as I could remember food and my avoidance of it had been dominating my existence. I felt fat. I felt stupid. I hated myself and all the time I was running scared. Convinced that nobody could possibly like me, I felt like the biggest failure on earth, and deserving nothing better I felt bad and guilty about everything. All of my life I'd had nothing to be anything other than happy about and I should have been happy, but I wasn't. I was desperately unhappy and I didn't know why. Completely out of control, my life didn't make sense anymore and I'd given up trying to understand why I should feel so bewildered and lost, when I'd always been the child who'd had everything.

Early Beginnings

Born one cold winter morning at North Tees General Hospital Stockton, in the November of 1968, I couldn't have wanted for a more comfortable start in life. Stable and conflict free, my life at home was a secure one and my surroundings were far luckier than most. Living on the edge of a green belt our house was ideally situated and I loved it. It was placed centrally in a small but lively cul-de-sac, and whilst the front of our house looked out over our road, the back spilled out over a grassed valley. Punctuated with trees and bushes and a beck which ran the full length of its base, the valley or 'field' as it was known, was an excellent place for kids to play, and I loved it. Providing us with all that we needed, playing on the field was something that my brother Gary and I took for granted and I happily recall spending days and days in the summer, exploring different parts of the field with the kids from our road.

Stomping through long grass, jumping the beck and plodging through the boggy bit, always there seemed to be something new to do and always I remember having good fun. Since there were few girls in our road, I played mainly with boys and, learning quickly to beat many of them at their own games, I found myself readily accepted. When it came to tree climbing, beck jumping and football, I was as agile as the best of them and secretly I enjoyed being good at things I wasn't supposed to be good at. I was pretty good at cricket and rounders as well, and I used to love watching the lads' faces each time I hit a ball further than they probably thought I could. And I guess now that that was actually quite important to me. Allowing me to feel different and a little out of the ordinary maybe, even as a tiny child, I suppose I loved to feel valued and in some way noticed.

Come winter, when the dark evenings and poorer weather conditions arrived, my friends from the road and I abandoned the field and moved indoors to one or another of our houses. Always made welcome by my parents, usually my brother and I and half the street would retire to our house, where we'd watch the television or play cards and other games – waiting for the snow to arrive. When the snow finally did come, we'd take once more to the field where we'd sledge from morning until night, dodging the beck and returning home drenched and shattered. I loved it when it snowed. Bringing with it a whole new set of games to play, snow gave my friends and I variety, and for that alone I welcomed it.

Sometimes I enjoyed being on my own when it snowed. Only when nobody else was around could I fully appreciate the beauty of a world transformed. A world turned black and white and without colour somehow seemed a less threatening one. Dulling the sharpness of voices, snow brought with it quietness and peace and I liked that. Being alone, being the only person occupying a particular part of the world at a particular point in time, promised uniqueness and a tranquillity which didn't seem possible when others were about. Uniqueness that set me apart from everyone else and uniqueness that felt safe. When I was on my own, time was mine and as far back as I can remember, I used to enjoy the freedom that that gave me.

During my earliest days, I found it easiest to satisfy my need for time alone, early in the morning before the rest of the house stirred. Especially at weekends, as this was the best time for me to play with the Lego and red plastic train set that I shared with Gary. On my own, I could do what I wanted to do. If I wanted to build seven little houses to go around a particular shaped track, I could build the track and position the houses where I wanted. Unlike when I played with other children, I didn't have to automatically go against my wishes and settle for something that I didn't want, purely because someone else came up with an alternative idea which I never felt able to argue against. When I was alone, I could make the decisions. Games were less complicated and I didn't have to worry about being bossy or greedy or selfish. (As far as I was concerned, being bossy or greedy was inexcusable and being selfish was one of the worst things that anybody could be.)

Come snow, rain or shine, at weekends Gary and I were always given the opportunity to choose things that we'd like to do. If we wanted to spend Sunday afternoon in the hills, my mum would pack a picnic and my dad would drive the four of us up into the Cleveland

Hills or the Yorkshire Dales. If we fancied a swim or a paddle in the sea, my dad would take us to the baths or we'd all go to the beach. If we wanted to feed ducks, play in the park or spot purple doors (I was obsessed with purple when I was two) we'd jump in the car and go. If it rained we'd go flood hunting. If it snowed we'd go drift hunting and on Saturdays, until I was ten, I was always taken to gymnastics. When we weren't out doing something at weekends, Gary and I would potter about at home playing with friends or 'helping' my parents in the garden or kitchen.

Nothing was ever too much trouble for my mum and dad and I both loved and appreciated everything that they did for Gary and I, that other parents didn't seem to do for their children. As kids, my brother and I were extremely lucky. Regardless of what we wanted to spend time doing, when my mum and dad were about, they'd always have the time and energy to do whatever. Whether they too enjoyed what Gary and I did I don't know, but if they didn't nothing was ever said and reasonable requests were seldom turned down. Completely unselfish, my parents were never unreasonable and would choose always to give their time rather than say 'no' – especially my dad. I don't think my dad ever said 'no'.

Occasionally at weekends and sometimes in the evenings, my dad would jump in the car and go off visiting families living on the other side of Stockton. Delivering messages and bits and pieces, often he'd take Gary and I with him for the ride. At home our road was quiet, uncluttered and homelike. In contrast to my image of what a road should be like, the streets I visited with my dad were very different. Isolated, bleak and kind of raw, they *felt* very different too. Streets and non-existent pavements littered with glass, child-broken bricks, destroyed fences, ripped cans, washing machines, chunks of metal and car tyres – sometimes smouldering. Houses with open doors and expertly boarded windows. Gardens full of bald and bitten dogs with ears missing. Cats with only three legs and hungry looking kids carving swords from new bits of fence.

Scary and yet amazing, the people who belonged to the houses were different too. Poorly understood and little respected by a life whose values conflicted sharply with their own, they were by social definition, alienated and alone. Encapsulated by a struggle for survival and fired by adrenaline, only an aggressive deviation made life possible and you could almost smell it. Hard and risky, life was without its comforts and, thin and pale, the people who my dad visited had every reason to hate and mistrust a society that began where their streets ended. But if they did, I never saw it. The insight I gained from driving around with my dad, showed me a different side to humanity. A humanity held together like no other. People thriving upon societal neglect, who'd do anything to help one another. People who very clearly loved my dad.

Always welcomed, whenever my dad turned into these scary scary roads, immediately half the street would rush out to greet him and often our car would be swamped by faces, young and old, which gradually became familiar to me. Whenever Gary or I were in the car with him, we too would be made to feel welcome – more perhaps than anywhere else we ever went. Accepted purely because my dad was my dad, I was always incredibly proud of what he obviously meant to the families that lived there. Equally respected by this particular set of people, my mum was as well regarded as my dad and she too would always be warmly greeted and immediately invited into house after house. But unlike Gary and I, my mum's acceptance was hers in her own right. Highlighting quality after quality that she shared with my dad, my mum also had something about her that set her apart from every other mum I knew.

Determined to make a difference in the lives of kids who had nothing, both my parents were extraordinary. Socially aware and of sound moral judgement, my mum and dad met on a youth-leaders' training course and before I was born they spent a lot of time together, doing voluntary work helping underprivileged kids in a Stockton youth club. Committing themselves to the needs of Stockton's neediest kids, for years my mum and dad provided the structure, stability, care and concern that these kids lacked, and without doubt they did make a difference. Fitting in well with what was going on around me, when I arrived in 1968, the youth club – also in its infancy – was probably helping to care for two dozen or so families. Working initially during evenings and at weekends, as the number of needy families identified increased, so too did the time and energy that my parents devoted to their needs. They were snowed under by growing responsibilities and club needs, and when it became apparent that part-time support was not enough to support the full needs of all the kids and their families, my dad (a chemical engineer with ICI) gave up his job for a year to run the youth club full-time instead. This allowed my mum to cut back on her involvement with club activities. I was probably about three then and my brother one.

At that time my dad concentrated intensively upon the needs of one group of eight young lads (in addition to running the club), and organised meetings, activities and holidays for the group whenever time allowed, whilst my mum continued to provide background support. Dad occasionally involved Gary and I in club activities and would sometimes bring the lads home to our house. As I grew up I was lucky enough to gain insight into the lives of kids from very different backgrounds to mine. This gave me a privileged insight, which I still value greatly and use today – insight which taught me far more than I realised at the time – especially about my parents. My mum and dad were more than just special. To me they were unique and I loved them dearly for the quality care and attention that they gave to kids who had nothing and nobody else.

Quietly gentle, easy going and highly respected outside of our house, at home my parents were just the same. They were fun loving and conflict free; the atmosphere in our house was usually laid back and relaxed, and friends were always welcome. Free, within reason, to do whatever we wanted, Gary and I were always treated fairly at home and I'm sure most of the time we were the envy of the kids in our road. Trusted with responsibility, our lives were never restricted by boundaries and I for one seldom felt hard done by.

The only rules in our house were to do with eating. My mum was concerned greatly with the health and well-being of my dad and keen to provide Gary and I with only the very best – she was obsessed with healthy eating. Vitamins and vegetables were encouraged, while sugary foods and fried meals were all but banned from our house. Mum was paranoid that one or other member of the family would develop heart disease or some form of cancer, and there was always something new that we were encouraged to force ourselves either to eat or cut from our diets completely. Cod-liver oil, beta carotene, yeast extracts, sunflower seeds, vitamin C, figs, dates... caffeine, saturated fats, sugar, sweets, biscuits, cakes, you name it – if we were to keep my mum happy we each knew exactly what to and what not to eat.

If a little controlling, my mum's attitude to health and eating affected us all, but for all the right reasons. Driven by concern and caring, it was also typical of her. Always thoughtful and always kind, my mum was the kind of person who would worry about and do what she felt to be the best for anyone. She was popular, friendly, had a good sense of humour and everyone liked her. Interested in people and politics and outraged by injustice, whilst she had no time for greed, selfishness and attention seekers, my mum was generous to a fault and would help anybody out. She was also tolerant and supportive of my dad's involvement with the club, and in between juggling the housework and bringing up my brother and I, she would always be there to deal with difficulties and problems that either my dad, the kids from the club or their families faced. Sharing with my dad a loving and argument-free relationship, my mum was bright and lively and seldom lost her temper.

Echoing many of my mum's qualities, my dad was a gentle giant as placid as the day was long. More like Mr Bean than Mr Bean himself, my dad was genuinely funny, almost to the point of not being able to help it. Even-tempered and a keen avoider of conflict, he was a thinker who always kept his thoughts to himself. A thinker who was quite difficult to get to know really. He was a man who was respected and highly regarded by everyone. A man at times so sensitive and perceptive that he seemed incredible. Often witty and always patient, my dad had time for anyone, and like my mum he did everything to maximise Gary's and my own chances for later success. Cheerful and happy, and not one to give himself a second thought, again like my mum, my dad would sooner see to the needs of others than sit and brood upon those of his own. And he never got angry. Or at least if he did he never let us know. In fact, I don't think he ever let any negative feelings show and come to think of it he wasn't the only one.

My dad wasn't the only one to put himself down rather than acknowledge his strengths and achievements either. We were all good at that in our house. Something else we were all good at at home was not expressing ourselves effectively. That's not to say that we didn't talk much as a family, because we did. What we seldom seemed to do was discuss anything personal on a deeper than everyday level. At least that was how I perceived things at the time. We all got on very well in our house and apart from the usual sibling squabbles, there was rarely any visible friction between us. Living with the philosophy that 'if you don't have something nice to say, say nothing', rather than ever voice an opinion which might upset, in our family much probably went unsaid. Certainly it did as far as I was concerned. Rather than confront a member of the family for upsetting or annoying me, usually I'd keep my feelings to myself. Scared that I might be seen to be 'bad' or 'not nice' if I lost my temper, I'd 'suck up to' and appease the person responsible instead, in the hope of stopping whatever from happening again. A pattern of behaviour which I used a lot, although it's difficult to tell whether my parents and Gary played the same 'pleasing' game too. I suspect that to varying degrees they did.

Definitely in our house there seemed to be a lot of conflict avoided. There must have been, because I seldom encountered it, and compared to other families, that seemed odd. Odd maybe but somehow safe and not something that I wanted to change. Not that my desires were particularly healthy. Although I for one always enjoyed the constant pleasantness that I found at home, maybe in some ways it prevented each of us from ever really knowing what anyone else was thinking or feeling. Despite probably causing all of us, at times, to have needs go unmet, the way in which we communicated as a family without doubt benefited me enormously. I was cushioned from nastiness and ill feelings and, whilst other kids struggled daily to survive battle-zone homes, neglect and abuse, my childhood was protected. It was also a happy one and one in which I felt safe – until I was about seven.

The gentle and uncomplicated childhood that I'd spent happily playing with other kids ended when, on reaching junior school, I entered a divided world where boys played only with boys and girls only with girls; a strange phenomenon which hadn't happened before.

This was a state of play which felt totally alien to me and one which I didn't like. Cliquey and back-stabbing, girls I decided could not be trusted, and I didn't want to keep their boring two-faced company. Forever falling out with one another whilst the boys got on with playing games and enjoying themselves, the people who surrounded me seemed intent only upon hurting and upsetting each other. Day after day there'd be tears and I hated it. It disturbed me too. Name-calling, bullying and exploitation. Why did girls have to be so cruel? Why? What did they get out of talking and laughing behind each others' backs? What was the point in making each other miserable when they could be having fun instead? To me none of this made sense. And as much as I tried to understand, I simply could not comprehend why my peers should treat one another so badly, so much of the time. Why couldn't everyone get on?

At the age of seven it had seemed simple to me. If everyone could just be nice to everyone else, the world would be a far better place and everyone would be happy. Certainly the playground would be a happier place. Nobody would be without friends, every child would have someone to play with and I for one, wouldn't have had to worry constantly about what others were saying about me when I wasn't there. But as much as I longed for peace in the playground, it never came and what I witnessed daily affected me deeply. Sickened by feelings of powerlessness, in not knowing how to stop the ignorance and cruelty before me, I became scared. Scared that I might become in some way unlikeable, scared that one day I might become the 'despised one' whose life would be made miserable by those I could not understand. Terrified that the inevitable would happen and most of the time paranoid that my 'friends' were already talking behind my back, I dreaded playtime. In fact I dreaded any time at school when we weren't all kept quiet. Only when there was silence could I assume that nobody was talking about me. If other kids were whispering, my mind could not settle until I knew for definite that I was not the subject. So convinced that people were laughing behind my back, I was even too scared sometimes to go to the loo. If I was sitting at a table or standing in the playground with two or more girls, I wouldn't dare leave for fear of them bitching about me in my absence.

Forever surrounded by other children, I think by definition I was popular at school but I never felt it. I was too busy back-watching to enjoy any kind of relationship, and was probably the most lonely 'popular' kid in the school. That was how I felt anyway. Totally alone. Alone and with no one to voice my fears to. Other girls couldn't be trusted. I didn't know any boys well enough. My teachers would never believe me and I didn't want to tell my mum and dad how I was feeling because I didn't want them to worry about me. I wasn't worthy of anyone's worry anyway and besides, really there was nothing to say. I didn't know that my fears were fears. I had no one else's thoughts to compare mine with and I had no reason to doubt that the thinking that dominated my life was any different from that which determined everybody else's. I certainly didn't know that what I was thinking was perhaps not normal. What I did know, however, was that I needed to be liked and by everyone. Only if nobody had any reason to victimise, pick on or talk about me, could I make sure that it wouldn't happen. Doubting that I was a likeable child, in order to survive my peers I decided that there was a lot of me that I needed to change. Privileged beyond just desserts, unattractive and a swot, selfish, boring and uninteresting; being myself could not possibly be good enough.

In order to be liked by everyone, I would need to behave so as to be liked by everyone. And if that meant throwing everything into making sure that those around me were forever happy, and happy with me, then so be it. Sensitive to the needs, hurt and upset of others anyway, all I had to do was look out for everyone else and make up for my own inadequacies by always putting other people before myself. Hiding negative thoughts towards others and positive thoughts towards myself, I decided my role in life was to be: happy, fun to be with, interesting and always smiling. Nothing less would do. Denying myself rights, wants and in fact everything that I needed in order to secure any kind of continued genuine happiness, I knew exactly what I had to do.

Forcing myself to be cheerful, thoughtful, kind and caring at all times and at all costs, I began trying to do nothing wrong. If I disagreed with someone else's opinion, I didn't say. When someone asked me to do something I didn't want to do, I did it. If faced with deciding what I wanted to do, instead of choosing something for me, I'd choose what I thought everyone else would like instead. During lessons if another child got stuck or wanted equipment, I'd help them out by either explaining answers or giving mine away along with my equipment. If somebody fell over in the playground, I'd be the first person there to make sure that they were OK. If I spotted someone else crying, I'd go over and ask what was wrong and I worried about everyone. Perhaps feeling sad and lonely myself, sometimes when I watched other kids in the playground I'd worry about whether they were happy or not. I hated seeing anyone unhappy, and in my mind I longed for playmates for the loners and friends for the friendless. I hated seeing other kids fall out as well and forever sitting on some fence or other, whenever my peers did break friends, it always seemed to be me that tried to rectify the hurt and repair the damage done.

I was desperate to be accepted and wanted by other kids, and there was probably nothing that I didn't try in order to be liked. But if constantly pleasing and keeping other people happy successfully stopped me from ever being a victim, it did nothing to boost the low opinion that I had of myself. Compared to others I had everything. My parents didn't fight, I had a roof over my head and my home was a stable one. I had clothes, toys and a bed I could call my own. At night I knew where I'd be sleeping, I knew where my parents were and in the morning when I awoke I knew that there'd always be food in the cupboards. I didn't have seven brothers and sisters to compete against for attention and affection, neither of my parents were dead or missing, and I faced before me a bright and promising future. But I wasn't happy. And that made me feel terrible. Not the unhappiness itself but the fact that I wasn't happy. How dare I not be? I had no right to be unhappy. I felt ungrateful and selfish: I didn't deserve anything and yet there was nothing that I didn't have. Worthless, my values didn't make sense and I felt bad. Bad and guilty. I should have been happy. Anybody else in my shoes would have been happy. Anybody half decent that is. But I wasn't happy and to me that was proof enough that I was being unreasonable and expecting too much.

How dare I want anything more? How dare I not be happy? Compared to the kids whose lives my parents tried to improve, my life was a dream – and yet still I wasn't satisfied. Unhappy and ungrateful, I couldn't possibly justify my inability to feel contented and I didn't like myself because of it. To be dissatisfied with everything that I had was awful and that meant that I was awful. A spoilt selfish brat. No wonder I was scared that people wouldn't like me if they knew what I was really like. There was nothing to like. Seeing traits in myself that I disliked in others, I felt vulnerable and somehow distanced from the kid I felt I should have been. Powerless to do anything other than continue trying to please, all I could do was smile and try harder. So I smiled and tried harder but still I felt alone. Yes, it was true that throughout my entire childhood no child ever broke friends with me – but no child ever made great friends with me either. As a kid I never had a best friend and that worried me constantly. I desperately wanted to be wanted and yet nobody seemed to want me. Not knowing why I'd never been chosen to be anybody's best friend, I could only conclude that either I was doing something wrong or that there was something wrong with me. I didn't know which of the two to blame. Both possibilities upset me. Popular and yet unwanted, there I was, the child who had everything but nothing that interested anybody. Empty and worthless, I wasn't just a failure – I was a first class one. Quite an achievement for a seven-year-old.

Taking my childhood thoughts and behaviours with me, in the September of 1980 I moved on from primary school and began attending The Grange, a comprehensive school that comprised approximately twelve hundred pupils. Whilst I settled quickly into the new routines of a new school, much of my life remained the same. Surrounded now by a larger crowd of faces, I suppose I made more friends in my first week at the school than ever before, and yet paradoxically I still felt isolated. I was growing more scared with age that anyone knowing the real me would reject me; still I kept myself distanced and still I remained frighteningly unaware that my thoughts, fears and consequent behaviours were not normal. Boring and unstimulating, my first two years at the school passed with little happening. Nothing exciting ever seemed to take place and apart from being able to recall that I started to plan everything that I said or did to ensure that I upset no one, in fact I can remember little else.

If I was aware then of any changes to the shape and size of my body, at that time they didn't bother me. I didn't fall into the trap of becoming obsessed by weight and eating until I returned to school in the autumn of 1982, for the beginning of the third year. Maybe a little too heavy for my thirteen years, maybe not. If I was to continue avoiding having any reason to be disliked or picked on, I reasoned that losing weight had for me become necessary. Beginning to eat less was therefore a conscious decision. Losing my mind and with it all excitement of life, however, was not. That was something that just happened. Quite simply, everything changed without me having the slightest idea as to what was taking place. As I tried (unsuccessfully at first) to lose the few pounds needed to free my mind of its fears, without warning I found myself controlled almost completely by replacement thoughts and fears which were so much more restricting than any I'd had before.

Fat-phobic, food-craving and weight-obsessed, as my mind very rapidly ceased functioning effectively it also ceased very rapidly being my own and I became trapped. Completely taken over by a non-functioning kind of existence, by the time I'd entered upper school and was preparing for my O-levels, I'd mastered the art of eating very little without anybody else knowing. I would sleep late so as to avoid breakfast at home; at school I began substituting lunch with a can of Diet Coke and a coffee, stating either that I wasn't hungry or that I'd never been one to eat much during the day. And nobody seemed to mind. In fact nobody seemed to notice, or at least if they did, they never said. Once home again, in the evenings I did eat but not with the family and I'd only ever touch foods that I'd prepared myself. Having become both 'vegetarian' and 'health-conscious', I managed to deceive my parents into believing that the huge pan of vegetables I ate each night for my evening meal was healthy. Rewarding me doubly, whilst the 'pan of veg' aspect of my dieting staved off suspicion regarding my not eating, in meeting with vitamin-boosting, fat-reducing delight, it also kept my mum happy.

The last thing I needed at that point was to lose my will-power but with time vegetables alone bored me and I began craving other foods. Odd foods that more and more I felt compelled at first to stare at and then to taste. Liquorice, cocoa powder and melon skins, dried

milk, raisins and soap bubbles, raw porridge oats and kitkats. I longed
for them all, especially the kitkats, and after a couple of months of
eating less than 300 calories a day, I found it impossible to think of
anything other than the cravings. Driving me to distraction, soon
after the cravings had set in I began nibbling or 'pinching' tiny
quantities of the non-vegetable foods that my body was being forced
to cry out for. Feeling very much a failure for being too weak willed
to keep my daily intake below 300 calories, it was probably the nibbling
that kept me sane and made it possible for me to sit and pass my O-
levels.

Disappointed (and disgusted with myself) at not having achieved
top grades in all of my O-levels, when I left school and moved on
to Stockton Sixth Form College, nothing could have quite prepared
me for the feelings of academic failure that I'd meet there. I was
unable to keep my thoughts on anything other than food, its forms
and its effects, and as my efforts to concentrate became more and
more futile I found myself completely unable to cope with my
studies. At school I'd been led to believe that I was easily bright
enough to pursue the career in medicine that I'd always wanted and
yet now, now my intelligence had gone. I couldn't understand why,
when I was working harder than ever before, I should find myself
getting nowhere. But I *wasn't* getting anywhere and my lack of ability
scared me. Helpless to do anything, as my grades dwindled quite
spectacularly I became more and more disheartened with everything
and I could see little point in carrying on. Thankfully at that time I
found myself surrounded by friends who, probably without realising,
gave me everything I needed and made life bearable – just.

Not realising that for years I had been depressed, I didn't finally
reach a point of realisation that there was anything really wrong
with me until one day during my first year at sixth form, when Roger
(who was later to become my partner) challenged me about my eating.

Roger was the first person who didn't *have* to love me who did. He
was the kindest person I'd ever known: always smiling, always happy
and impossible not to notice. From the very moment we met I could
tell that there was a caring about him. A devoted and intelligent caring
that gave me strength and confidence. A caring which warmed and

welcomed me and told me so much about the friend who would become much more than a friend, and more, even, than that.

Probably the brightest person I'd ever met, I first got to know Roger in the September of 1985. He was surrounded constantly by friendly banter, laughter and old school friends all seemingly enjoying themselves, and within a day or two of knowing him I knew that I wanted him as a friend. Introduced properly by Caryn (a friend of his from school who I'd got to know through hockey), immediately Roger and I hit it off together and more or less straight away we became very good friends. Roger and Caryn changed my experience of life, as they then introduced me to their friends from school and every one of them welcomed me to join them and, at the very time that I needed it most, I found myself belonging to a set of people who really seemed to care about me. People who tried always and succeeded often to make me feel respected, valued and better about myself than I did: and people whose love of life and love of me gave me reason to fight on.

Creating the beginnings of a support system that would carry me through the next ten years, as my friends and I grew closer and closer, so too did Roger and I. Roger was often more aware of what I was experiencing than I was myself, and even when I didn't realise that I wasn't happy, Roger seemed able to sense it and he'd always do something about it. Usually he'd say something to make me smile or he'd do something to make me laugh. Sometimes he'd pick me up and twirl me round and round until we both fell over, or he'd fling me over his shoulder and run off with me until he could carry me no further. Sometimes he'd tickle me, or he'd catch hold of my arms and waltz me (under fake protest) round the college floor. Often he'd just give me a hug.

Letting me know that he'd always be there for me, there was never a moment when Roger let me down and never a moment when he was around that I didn't feel special. Supportive of every thought that I had and every thing that I did, like no one else he loved me and like no one else I loved (and needed) him. Forever patient and understanding, regardless of what my changing moods threw at him, whenever he was with me I felt safe and secure. Protected somehow from a world I didn't understand and a life that I felt sometimes didn't even exist. Wrapped up and adored, appreciated and taken care of, when I was with Roger I felt together. Without him I felt lost.

Classically tall, darkly handsome and wonderful with small animals, tiny children, washing machines, tin openers, water pistols… there was nothing about Roger that wasn't appealing and nothing that I didn't love. Completely incapable of getting through a day without something unfortunate, smelly, sticky, painful or brown happening to him, just by being himself Roger could lift my mood and make me laugh, and I valued that so much in him.

The only person I'd ever met who had managed to get bitten by four different living things (ant, spider, dog, horse) during one two-week holiday, Roger was somehow unique. Predictable only in being completely unpredictable, he was one of those people that things just seem to 'happen' to and I loved him dearly for it. I never quite knew what would happen to him next. Whether he was dropping a full plate of fish, chips, tomato sauce and vinegar all over my parents' brand new pale green carpet; accidentally sneezing treacle into the grooves of his sister's favourite album; snapping the accelerator pedal of my dad's car (twice), or being struck on his head by a flying pork pie on his first day at work as a holiday postman, there was always something about him to tease me away from myself. And I needed that.

Distracting me from the crap thoughts and scary nothingness that threatened to consume me, with Roger I felt alive and free almost to be myself – and I needed that too. I needed his determination to make my day – every day – as well, and his ability to get me to see things differently and more positively. But perhaps more than anything at the time, I needed his constant strivings to make my life fun and as laughter filled as possible. Teaching me more about love than anything or anybody else, just knowing someone as patient and as sensitive as Roger made a difference. Knowing that he chose to spend most of his time doing everything to make me happy, meant everything to me.

Unable to see at first that Roger was aware of the eating difficulties that I wasn't sure I had, it was a while before I realised just how important Roger was to me. The first person to ever express concern over my eating, Roger was also the first to prove that he wouldn't think any less of me if I admitted what was really going on. Having been worried about me for a while, by the time he finally did confront me with his concerns about my not eating and weight loss, I was exhausted of life. I felt completely helpless and devoid of hope. I'd lost any sense of confidence that I might once have had and I was paranoid that people were looking at me, disgusted that I could have let myself get so fat. I needed to be liked by everyone and yet I hated myself. I despised my body for being my body and I could not forgive my mind for not being intelligent enough to override my difficulties. And since everything I did had to be perfect, I was also successful at nothing.

My weight had fallen from probably just under nine stone to just over six, I'd become addicted to Diet Coke and I was exercising obsessively. During the day I was jogging and forcing myself to do five hundred sit-ups; at night I was running up and down the stairs two hundred times or more. Feeling fat all the time, I could no longer cope with eating more than 600 calories a day and for as long as I could remember I'd been wishing time away constantly, depending upon what I had or had not eaten. At night I found it difficult to sleep. In the mornings I was waking early, and all the time my extremities were blue and I was freezing. Terrified of gaining weight, I was weighing myself up to fifteen times a day and I felt guilty about everything that I ate.

Obsessed with food, I'd taken to wandering around shops gaining pleasure from staring at, picking up, running my fingers over and then putting back, the fat laden chocolate bars which I'd banned myself from eating. I'd begun too to gain an empty satisfaction from watching other people eat the foods that I denied myself and oddly I felt more restrained, and in some ways almost a better person, for having the will to not eat when other people didn't.

Twisted and destructive, my thoughts were anything but normal and yet I couldn't see it. All I could see was a 'fat' self. A self which to me was worthless and valueless, a me which felt nothing but ugly and huge. Crying myself to sleep every night and dreading every next day, before I was eighteen I'd reached a point where I could cope no more. Disillusioned with both myself and life in general, if tomorrow meant another day of 'feeling fat', I didn't want tomorrow to come. I wanted to die.

Empty Words

'Clare I love you, I love you so much and I'm scared. I don't want to lose you but I can see that you're starving yourself. You're making yourself ill Clare, you know you are. You're anorexic aren't you? Please will you see a doctor? Nothing would make me happier than if you did.' Roger

'I can't believe you don't like yourself Clare. How can you possibly get up on a morning and not like who you are? You're the kindest, most sensitive and caring person I know. You're funny, you're witty and you always cheer me up. You're brilliant Clare, you're my best friend and I love you. Why can't you see how special you are?' Caryn

'You're lovely as you are Clare, you don't need to lose weight.' Nick

'You worry me sometimes Lindsay. You've got to eat. I'm not letting you out of this shop until you've bought something to eat.' Chris

'Are you shivering? Here have my jumper. Why don't you eat just a little bit more, if only to keep you warm? It wouldn't hurt really would it and if it stopped you turning blue, it would have to be better than this wouldn't it?' Ravi

'How can you say that you're not anorexic when all you've had to eat today is an apple and that's your ninth can of Diet Coke?' Roger.

'I'm worried about you Clare, you look ill.' Caryn

'How can you think you're fat, there's nothing on you?' Scott

'Clare you're gorgeous, absolutely gorgeous. You're small, waif-like, you're blonde, you've got cheek bones, everything. You're young, you're pretty, you're intelligent,

you've got everything going for you. You're beautiful, you're bloody petite. How can you hate yourself? You're gorgeous Clare – you just are.' Chris

'Clare you need help. It breaks my heart to see you doing this to yourself, please will you go and see your doctor?' Roger

I spent the first five years of my anorexia in denial. At least I think it was denial. As hard as Roger and my friends tried to convince me that I wasn't fat, that I wasn't the awful person that I perceived myself to be, but that I did have a problem, I couldn't believe them. How could I when I had all the evidence I needed to prove otherwise?

Maybe it was confusion that stopped me from seeing myself in the way that my friends stated everyone else did. Maybe my thoughts had become too muddled for me to make sense of them anymore. Quite what was really going on in my head at the time I honestly don't know, but nothing that anyone said to me could convince me that I was anorexic. What I do know is that by the time Roger and my friends were trying to convince me that I was anorexic, I knew as much about anorexia as there was to know. Unhappy and obsessed with losing weight, I *longed* to be anorexic. To 'lose my appetite' and with it the fatness that I was desperate to shift, *without effort*, was my idea of bliss. I really believed (as most eating disordered people do) that being anorexic would solve everything and for years I'd scoured book shops up and down the country, desperate to read anything about the illness that I so much wanted but hadn't got. Envious of those who had been lucky enough to develop anorexia, in reading about their experiences, I genuinely didn't recognise that the symptoms that diagnosed them equally diagnosed me. Maybe this in itself was the most telling symptom of all.

Even Roger couldn't get me to see that I was anorexic. Pushing our relationship to the edge, after trying everything to wake me up to the fact that I had a genuine problem, eventually he sat me down one night and just fired the following questions at me:

'Clare, are you terrified of gaining weight?'

'Yes.'

'Do you think you're fat even though you know weight charts tell you you're underweight?'

'Yes.'

'Do you relentlessly pursue thinness through starvation?'

'Yes.'

'Have you experienced significant weight loss?'

'Yes.'

'Have your periods stopped or become irregular?'

'Yes.'

'Are you scared of maintaining a normal body weight for your height?'

'Yes.'

'Do you sometimes vomit, purge or exercise excessively to avoid gaining weight?'

'Yes.'

'Are you obsessed with food, weight and calories, and do these thoughts occupy your mind most of the time?'

'Yes.'

'Do you avoid social situations which might involve food?'

'Yes.'

'Do you feel guilty when you eat?'

'Yes.'

'Do you experience any of the following:
– extreme sensitivity to cold, poor circulation and skin discoloration
– sleep disturbance
– hyperactivity and restlessness
– perfectionist traits and obsessive behaviours
– loss of sexual drive
– growth of downy hair all over the body
– mood swings and irritability?'

'Yes.'

'Is your self-esteem low?'

'Yes.'

'Are you anorexic?'

'No.'

'Have you just answered these questions defensively?'

'Yes.'

'Does that not tell you something?'

'No.'

'Clare, have you or have you not just admitted that you have all the symptoms of anorexia?'

'Suppose so.'

'Clare, are you anorexic?'

'No.'

It was perhaps significant that I chose the next day to stop going out with Roger. Exactly what I was running from I don't know but I still couldn't accept that I was anorexic. Even when Roger and I were back together again and he got really upset again, I couldn't see that I had an eating disorder that was dominating my life. OK, yes, I was obsessed with dieting and yes, I was trying to improve my low self-esteem by losing weight and becoming more 'wantable', but that didn't mean I was anorexic. Anyone my size would have done the same. Nowhere in any of the books I'd read, were symptoms described as trivial as I perceived mine to be. In my eyes therefore, if the books were to be believed, any 'symptoms' that I had could hardly be considered serious enough to even be symptoms.

As far as I was concerned, if answering 'yes' to all of Roger's questions meant without doubt that I was anorexic then that made me a fraud, because I wasn't anorexic. I couldn't be. To be anorexic (as everything I read seemed to confirm) I would need to weigh less than four stone and be near to death in hospital, eating nothing at all. And since I satisfied none of these requirements, there was my proof. No matter what Roger and my friends said or did to convince me otherwise, I genuinely believed that I was not anorexic and I genuinely believed that I was not worthy of anyone's care and attention. The words of those watching me were empty words. They didn't mean anything to me.

Desperately in need of help, all I thought I was, was a failure.

Had I known then that the vast majority of anorectics do not exhibit symptoms as serious as the 'worst case scenarios' documented in the literature, and had I been aware that it is possible to be anorexic even at normal body weight, maybe I would have realised I had a 'real' problem long before I eventually did. Had I known too that 'feeling a fraud' about symptoms 'not serious enough to warrant the diagnosis of anorexia' is itself an important symptom of anorexia, that also might have helped me recognise that I was indeed anorexic.

For the diagnostic criteria of anorexia nervosa and bulimia nervosa see Appendix 1
For proof that you don't need to be on death's door to deserve and receive help see Appendix 2

PART TWO

Asking for Help

If it took me more than five years to admit to myself that I had a problem with my eating, it took Roger two years of constant gentle pestering to persuade me that I needed to see a doctor. And even then I remained unconvinced that my difficulties warranted medical attention.

Telling myself that I was going to settle Roger's mind, when I did finally take myself to my GP, I couldn't help but feel that I'd be wasting his time. I had no idea what I was going to say to him and I felt guilty about being there when really there was nothing wrong with me. Compared to everyone else in the waiting room I was perfectly healthy. I wasn't coughing or spluttering, I wasn't old or damaged or covered in a rash. I was fine. I might have looked a little nervous but apart from that there was nothing visible for anyone to see that would indicate that I had any reason to be there.

Scared that I couldn't think of an intelligible way of expressing what I wasn't sure I wanted to say, the longer I sat in the waiting room the greater my self-doubts grew. What was I going to say? What if I couldn't explain my presence? What reason did I have for being there? Did I have a reason? What if I was right and there was nothing wrong with me, and what if my doctor thought my symptoms were as trivial as I did? What if he got angry with me for wasting surgery time, what would happen then? Everyone would think I was stupid and that I'd made everything up to seek attention. Nobody would believe me, everyone would hate me and I'd feel even more awful. And then what would I do? Roger would know then that I was a fraud and then he'd hate me and…

Worried that I wouldn't be able to convince my GP that the symptoms that worried Roger did exist, I wanted to run. I didn't feel worthy of anybody's time and I desperately wanted to avoid the reaction that I believed my triviality would provoke. But for some stupid reason when I tried to get up to walk out, I found myself unable to move. I was rooted rigidly to the chair beneath me without knowing why I felt terrified, and yet almost as soon as

I walked into the consulting room, I knew that I was doing what I should have done long before.

I was also extremely lucky in that I found myself talking to a doctor who was not only sympathetic, but who appeared also to understand and accept everything that I managed to say. I hadn't spoken or cried about my anorexia with anyone besides Roger up until that point. But if at first I found it difficult to explain all that I perceived to be happening to me, I didn't find it difficult to cry and somehow that seemed strangely significant to me. Bringing down my defences, my tears brought with them permission to speak and although much of what I said probably lacked clarity, at last I found myself able to talk freely about everything that had been upsetting me.

Assuring me that he knew of many young people who had overcome difficulties similar to mine, having already examined my state of mind, Dr Ashford then examined my throat, neck and abdomen, and took blood for thyroid function and hormonal studies. Asking me to return to see him after my blood test results had been determined, although he didn't once use the word *anorexia,* I'm pretty sure he suspected it and before I left he suggested that I might benefit from seeing a psychologist. Having spent more than forty minutes of his time with me, as I walked from his room Dr Ashford smiled and thanked me for coming. Daring not to look at the frustration of faces that had accumulated behind me, I felt valued in that my worries had been taken seriously. I also sensed that I had aroused very real concern and it was probably then that I realised that I hadn't wasted anybody's time.

Roger was ecstatic when I told him that I'd finally been to see my doctor about my eating. Grabbing hold of me and lifting me in his arms, he sprang about his parents' living room like a kid on hot pins on Christmas morning – taking me with him. Completely overwhelmed, I felt as though I'd given him a far bigger present than he'd ever had before and that felt good. Had I needed reassurance that seeking help had not been a selfish thing to do, I needed it no longer. Roger had been genuinely worried about me and now for the first time I could actually see it. Happier and more relaxed than he had been in months, ironically, it wasn't until I saw worry drop from his face that I realised just how worried he had been.

I was pleasantly shaken by Roger's reaction to my seeking help, and once his excitement had warn off, the implications of what I'd done for me slowly began to dawn and I felt enormous relief. Everything now seemed more real and I felt less confused. I still didn't know what exactly was happening to me, but I could sense that I was moving forward as opposed to going nowhere, and that brought a welcome change. Feeling secretly pleased with myself for plucking up enough courage to ask for help, when I later told Caryn and Chris what I'd done, I became aware that Roger wasn't the only one who'd been concerned about me.

Caryn and Chris had also been worried by how little I was eating for quite a while. They'd both noticed and become concerned about how thin I'd become and although neither of them had ever said that they thought I was anorexic, with hindsight I suspect now that they knew. Certainly looking back I don't think that there was a day that went past when one or other of them didn't try to convince me that I wasn't fat and that I could do with eating more. Always protective of me, whilst Chris cracked endless crap 'Hardwick jokes' to gently highlight how thin and tiny I'd become, Caryn would comment often upon how cold and ill and blue I looked. They were demonstrating what I took to be a kind of caring, long before the two of them got to know me properly and, along with Roger, they were making a huge difference in my life.

Caryn belonged to the same set of friends as Roger, and was probably the first person I met at sixth form who I wanted to get to know better. Meeting her in the middle of a hockey field, knee deep in mud on the first Wednesday afternoon of term, straight away I'd liked her. Mud-flicking and mischievous, full of life and game for anything – there was just something about her that drew me towards her. Caryn was popular and always at the centre of whatever was going on; she was confident and strong, and the very kind of appealing person I'd always wanted to be. She was funny, she was witty, she had a good sense of humour and she had the uncanny knack of always making me feel better about myself whenever I was with her. And she could read me like a book. Finding in her qualities I'd never met in any female before her, at times she seemed to know me better than I did myself and usually she could tell exactly what was going on in my head, often long before I did.

Seeing well beyond the false smiles that held my life together, regardless of whether I felt fat, depressed or just pissed off, she could always detect whichever and she always seemed to know exactly what to do to pick me up again. When my self-esteem was low she'd boost it, when I was low she'd boost me. If I doubted my abilities she'd spell them out to me. If I needed to talk she'd know when to come and find me, and when words couldn't touch me she'd know when to give me a hug instead. She'd also detect when I needed time alone and somehow she seemed always to know when to leave me be. When I felt sad she'd say something to make me laugh or she'd do something daft (like sending me funny postcards or black midget gems through the post) to put a smile on my face again. If I put myself down, she'd jump on my negativity and bombard me instead with positive affirmations. If ever I was bored or unhappy, like Roger she'd do something mad or zany to bring me back to life and if ever I needed fun or excitement she'd create it around me. Often during the breaks at college she'd throw water or coffee over one of the lads, or she'd run off with something belonging to one of them, knowing full well that I could never resist joining in to 'help' her and that I loved the resulting fights and chases as much as she did. When I said how much I hated myself she'd say how much she loved me, and like no one else, when I felt fat she could motivate me – from even the 'fattest' of moods – into enjoying something. Caryn was just one of those people and I always felt incredibly lucky to have her around.

Friendly, caring and totally accepting of everything that I was, in Caryn I had everything that anyone could ever need in a friend and much much more. And she meant the world to me. Inspiring, motivating and helping me far more than she'll ever know, Caryn was just Caryn. She was also, and still is, the best friend I'd never had.

Caryn was also the person responsible for introducing me to Roger and Chris, and the circle of friends they shared from school who welcomed me to join them in everything they did at sixth form.

Complementing Roger and Caryn perfectly in terms of providing me with the love and support that I needed at the time, Chris was another good friend who always seemed to have time for me whenever I needed it. Meeting him probably on the same day that Caryn had introduced me to Roger, although it took me a little while to get to know Chris, I quickly grew to like him.

As gentle and as sensitive as anyone I knew, Chris was six-foot-seven, highly intelligent and completely mad. Sitting behind me and next to Roger in biology, he was witty, fun to be around and almost always in some sort of trouble with Roger in class. Attracting chaos and continuous activity, with a mind that never stopped firing, Chris made me feel alive. Alive and somehow valued, shaken into involvement and accepted just for being; alive and yet exhausted.

A good-time person and not afraid at times to be a bit of a lad, Chris was the sort of person who'd pick me up (mid pub, park or lecture) by my ankles and dangle me upside down – because he could. Monster. A big daft lad who'd do anything, it seemed, to attract and generate good times around him, in Chris I saw a mate who lived loudly to be laddish, but also a friend perhaps as sensitive (and vulnerable even) as me.

Giving out to me a side of him which he maintained nobody else ever saw, when I needed someone to talk to, Chris would sit for hours just listening. Putting his arm round me when I couldn't stop shaking, when words brought sense and logic he'd use them. When they didn't and I couldn't be reasoned from wanting to be dead, sometimes he'd just hug me. Watching out for me in much the same way he did his own two sisters, long before I was aware of his kindness towards me, Chris was like a brother to me. A brother, determined, it seemed, to keep me from hurting; a big brother who seemed almost to need to protect me as much as I needed protecting.

Whether he was aware fully of what was going on regarding my anorexia I don't know, but whenever I was at my lowest or felt at my fattest, it seems now that Chris always noticed. Taking me under his wing in many ways (maybe because of my anorexia, maybe not), he'd notice when I was at my most vulnerable and often I'd find myself protected from vulnerabilities I wasn't even aware of. If the paths were icy Chris would point out the slippy bits to me. If I stumbled on a climbing frame or got stuck on a rock, he'd grab me and lift me to ground before I ever fell. If I ran down a steep hill, he'd somehow be there in place to catch me if I tripped or couldn't stop, and if ever anybody commented on anything to do with me and size or weight, he'd always make sure that he or Roger had the last complimentary word.

Giving me everything and certainly all that I needed, together Roger, Caryn and Chris were the first people who really made me feel that I was worth something. Creating around me (despite my anorexia) the happiest days I'd known, to me there seemed to be something incredibly precious between the four of us. A bond between friends – strengthened for me by my illness – which gathered up my weaknesses and vulnerabilities and made me feel safe. A bond between friends whose love, strength and caring moved way beyond the realms of just friendship: together we shared a belonging. A special belonging which gave my life reason and which protected me from myself, and a belonging which gave me the confidence to improve my life by extending my trust to others. And certainly that was what happened.

As I grew to know and love Roger, Caryn and Chris, I very quickly found myself surrounded by an extended set of friends who generated around me all the distraction I needed. Accepting me as if they'd known me for years, Ravi and Nick, Scott, Chris and Andrew couldn't have welcomed me more warmly, and often because of them I felt the luckiest person at college. Making me feel valued and wanted, together with Roger, Caryn and Chris, my friends at sixth form secured my sanity and gave me the one thing I needed. At a time when I felt I deserved everything but, they made me feel special and I'll always love each one of them for it.

When I did eventually tell Caryn and Chris that I'd finally been to see my GP about my eating, I could tell from their reactions that they appreciated how difficult it had been for me to admit that perhaps there was something wrong. Grabbing me immediately and swinging me round and round, whilst Caryn yelled 'Excellent, well done, I'm so pleased, excellent, excellent' or something, Chris for once was gob-smacked and didn't seem to know what to say. Admitting to Roger later that he wished he'd said how brilliant he thought it was that I'd finally gone to get help, although he didn't actually say anything to me at the time, he indicated his support afterwards by being more attentive than usual – for ages. Encouraging me no end that I'd definitely done the right thing, despite their very different ways of showing it, I could tell that Caryn and Chris were as pleased as Roger had been that I'd at last recognised my eating as a problem, and suddenly I felt much less alone.

But if the support of my friends lifted my spirits, my blood test results did not. Dashing my hopes that my slowed metabolism (whether perceived or real) might be drug treatable, rather than detecting an underactive thyroid, instead my test results confirmed what deep down I'd known all along. The cause of my slowed metabolism was my restricted eating. The root of my problems therefore were not of physiological origin and drugs could not help me. Feeling angry that my body was functioning too correctly, I felt totally disillusioned with myself and pretty much hopeless. Sensing my disappointment, Dr Ashford picked up on a few alternative options still open to me and together we decided that I should be referred to an endocrinologist at North Tees General Hospital.

An appointment was made for me for September 12th, 1988 and again I met with a friendly man who did his best to quash my anxiety. Having introduced himself, he invited me to sit down and asked me to tell him why I'd been referred to see him. He then spent half an hour asking me questions, during which time my weight, my fears, my general health and that of my family, all came under close scrutiny. He then asked to examine me, took my pulse and blood pressure, looked thoroughly into my eyes, examined my chest, heart and abdomen, checked the circulation in my hands and feet, tested my reflexes, and measured my height. Next he asked me to define anorexia* for him. Thinking this a little odd given that he was the doctor and me the patient, without really thinking I parroted out the definition that Roger had fed me with his questions. Asking me to then stand on the scales, as he recorded my weight he fed back to me *his* definition of anorexia. Repeating almost word for word the exact definition that I'd given him, finally he then told me in no uncertain terms that I was anorexic.

Explaining that my body was running on extremely low reserves, as Dr Ashford had done before him, he suggested that I should be referred to a psychologist and asked me how I felt about the idea. The stigma attached to seeing a psychologist (or psychiatrist for that matter) did not worry me in the slightest and whereas I was the first to admit that I had refused to accept my anorexia, now in finally having it diagnosed, as though my hellish existence had at last been recognised, I felt more relieved than anything else. Aware also that my difficulties were now documented as 'real', in no longer perceiving everything as just a figment of a fattening imagination, strangely I felt less stupid than I had before. Medical help no longer intimidated me. I had just about enough confidence to pursue whatever channels were deemed necessary to overcome my eating problems and if that meant seeking psychiatric assistance, as far as I was concerned, then so be it.

That said however, it wasn't until the following February that I first saw a psychiatrist. Having secured a college place at York, since I had only two weeks left in Stockton before leaving home, it was decided that my initial referral should be put on hold temporarily to allow me the chance to settle in York before taking anything further.

*For clinical definition of anorexia (and bulimia) see Appendix 1
 For Roger's definition through questions see **Empty Words**

Dreading and then hating the uncertainty of a new beginning spent in new surroundings and with new people, I had neither the enthusiasm nor the confidence to enjoy myself in York. Living in student halls of residence with little time to myself, limited privacy and immense paranoia, I found college life pretty stressful. I despised being surrounded by what seemed like endless gossip, and, fearing that people would talk about me, I quickly learnt to keep myself to myself wherever possible. I missed Roger terribly and although I tried to convince myself with false smiles that I was enjoying student life, I wasn't happy at all.

When after a few months nothing seemed to improve and my eating became even more erratic, I made an appointment with Dr. Markham, a GP attached to the college, to ask if he would refer me to a psychiatrist in York. Not quite knowing what to expect from medical people now that I was officially anorexic, before I met Dr. Markham for the first time I dreaded to think what his reaction towards me would be. Convinced that the GP willing to take on the demands of the stereotypical anorectic would be a rarity, I half expected him to treat me with the impatience and annoyance that I'd been led to believe anorectics tend to provoke. I didn't even know whether he (or any doctor) would agree to take me as a patient and that prospect worried me – albeit needlessly as it turned out.

On meeting Dr. Markham, I found that I didn't receive the reaction that I'd been waiting for. As I described my history and explained why I'd come to see him, he invited me to talk further, smiled a lot and agreed straight away to refer me to a psychiatrist in York. Explaining what I might expect to gain from such a referral, Dr Markham spoke with genuine concern, told me that he would support me as best he could and welcomed me to call back any time that I needed to talk to someone. A man so quietly polite and impeccably spoken that he had reminded me of Tristan Farnon of *All Creatures Great and Small* fame, instantly I'd liked him and, therapeutic in its own right, his gentle manner had won my trust.

Feeling decidedly happier and closer to any sense of progress than I had before, that evening I phoned Roger to tell him of my referral. I also wrote to Caryn and Chris, not only to tell them that I now accepted that I was anorexic, but more importantly to let them know that I was doing something about it. Having chosen not to speak in detail about my anorexia with either of them before, now I very much wanted to. I was also dying to see Roger and to see his reaction to the progress that I felt I'd made, but for that I'd have to wait.

Separated by the 250 miles between York and Dundee and our respective colleges, for up to three or four weeks at a time I could only contact Roger by phone. Not used to him not being constantly around, speaking long distance on the phone had become a poor second best to seeing him every day and as time dragged on I found myself missing him more and more. But if the time we spent apart was awful, meeting up and being together again at weekends did in part make up for what I lost when Roger wasn't with me. Looking forward to our next few days together was at times the only thing that kept me going in York. Without them, and without Roger's constant love and support, I don't know what I'd have done.

I really missed my friends from home too, and as the last few weeks of my first term at college drew slowly to an end, I couldn't wait to get home. I was dying to feel part of things again, and Roger and I spent our first night back together in the pub talking, laughing and catching up with everyone.

I told Caryn everything about myself that evening and when a couple of nights later Chris took me to one side at The Kirk (a local night-club) and asked me how I was regarding the anorexia, I finally confided in him too. Nobody besides Roger had had the courage to ask me directly about my anorexia before and although at first I didn't really know how to respond to being confronted by someone else using the word 'anorexia', Chris couldn't have been more understanding and I gained a great deal from talking with him. Like Caryn, I could trust him implicitly and as I talked with him I could tell that his caring was genuine. Like Caryn also, there was much he didn't know about me and much I wanted to tell, and as I recall we sat for hours trying to make sense of what neither of us could. But it didn't really matter that my irrationality was beyond him. For years it had eluded both myself and Roger, and now it was beyond Caryn too. What really mattered to me was that now I had three people around me, willing not only to listen to me and to offer support if I needed it, but willing also to care about me with no conditions attached. That they each thought enough of me to do so, meant more to me than anything.

Feeling accepted and valued, I spent most of my first college break reliving and enjoying the times at home that I missed so much in York. As usual however, Christmas Day, the most absurd day of the year when by tradition everyday life grinds to a halt and chocolate dictatorship takes over, annoyed me. Inescapably surrounded by calories in every imaginable shape and form, my torturous thoughts as though given the day off, gave way to reality and tantalised my ever sharpened senses beyond all comprehension. Divine intervention had never particularly impressed me, nor done anything for me, and in being just one crazy, crazy day, Christmas meant nothing to me. I hated having to be happily part of everybody else's illusion and although I enjoyed spending time with my family, all day long I longed for the food to be eaten and the day to be gone.

But if I despised Christmas, our dog Alf loved it and I remember being woken on Boxing Day to the sound of him bounding into my room. Having secretly passed numerous chocolates and toffees in his direction the day before, I strongly suspect that the beginning of his canine devotion had been firmly cemented then. And since food and eating played almost as big a part in Alf's life as they did mine, it came as little surprise to me that as I tried to rid the house of it's festive edibles, I gained a rapidly expanding four-legged friend who followed me everywhere.

Driving back to York with the Christmas holidays behind me, having lost Roger to Dundee again and with three months of college life ahead of me, I found myself wondering why I was bothering to return. Hiding behind a sensible but boring exterior that kept me out of strife and made me unattractive as regards potential scandal, with little faith in my ability to cope away from home, I withdrew further into myself, lost all spontaneity and confidence and my sense of humour remained undetected. Days seemed to go on forever and ever and I started the beginning of 1989 feeling very low indeed.

Seeing a Psychiatrist

My first appointment with a psychiatrist had been made for February 12th, 1989. I didn't in any way feel ashamed of needing psychiatric help, nor did I feel any lesser a person because of it. In succumbing to a number of dreams however, I did begin to doubt the person that I believed other people would perceive me to be and as the 12th approached I decided to tell nobody in York where I was going. Giving some half-baked excuse which did not involve seeing a psychiatrist, when the day of my appointment did finally dawn, I took the morning off college and drove myself to the hospital.

Sitting in the waiting area, I nervously thumbed through magazines, reading articles about fishing and car maintenance that didn't interest me in the slightest but gave my brain something to do. I also found myself watching everyone else and to my horror, my mind, as guilty as the next person's, drove enormous energy into judging and making assumptions about everybody around me. Realising that I was doing myself the one thing that I'd hoped nobody would do with me, I sat wondering and worrying about the image that I was portraying until I could stand my doubts no more. Nervously trying not to appear tense I began counting the flowers on the wallpaper and then the tiles on the floor. Finally I concentrated on the nameplate on the closed wooden door in front of me, willing it not to open.

When the door did open, the young man who called my name and met me bore no resemblance to the psychiatrist type that I had imagined. Not that much older than me, he welcomed me through to his office with a smile and introduced himself as Dr Underwood, Senior House Officer to the lady consultant that I'd meet once he had taken down my history. For over an hour Dr Underwood fired questions at me, scribbling notes constantly throughout. He asked me of my fears and feelings around eating and weight control. He asked me how I viewed life, what I enjoyed and what I didn't. He got me to describe a typical day. He asked for my thoughts about the future and what I thought about myself. Then he asked me if

I'd ever thought about killing myself. A question that I'd never been asked before, completely thrown, I don't think I answered him. When he asked me the same question again and I noticed a change in the tone of his voice, I think for the first time I detected the full depth of my predicament.

Later the same morning when I went in to see the consultant, I was to be taken aback again. Explaining the complex nature of anorexia nervosa regarding treatment, she spelled out to me that since my eating had been disordered for over seven years, I had a huge problem on my hands which would be extremely difficult to solve. Stressing that I would need to fully commit myself to getting better, she warned me that the going would be tough, told me that I needed to take anti-depressants and said that she wanted me to attend a day hospital in York.

Having never considered myself in need of 'happy pills' before, when I refused to accept that I needed them, I was told quite simply that without anti-depressants I was of too low a mood to even enter into further treatment. Scared that it should seem necessary to prescribe me drugs for depression, I remained unconvinced that this course of action would do anything for me. Switching my thoughts instead to the day hospital part of the consultant's plan, although again I couldn't see how such therapy might benefit me, the idea at least seemed reasonable. Or it did, until I realised that I'd have to attend hospital all day every week day for about six months. Instantly unacceptable to me, I decided there and then not to go. Anyway it would be impossible.

To attend the day hospital with that degree of commitment I'd need to abandon my studies for a while, I'd risk getting kicked off my course for being mentally unstable and I'd have to tell my parents. And that would mean explaining everything because, as far as had been possible, I'd kept everything from them. Believing that what they didn't know couldn't hurt them, my parents didn't know that from the age of thirteen I'd been obsessed with abusing food and lowering my weight. They weren't aware that I was depressed and that I often contemplated suicide. I hadn't told them that I couldn't cope with my life and that I was desperately unhappy. They didn't know that I'd been seeing a psychiatrist and that now I needed months of full-time psychiatric treatment. My parents didn't even know that I'd been diagnosed as being anorexic. I hadn't wanted to worry them.

I'd also chosen not to tell my parents anything because I was too ashamed to admit to them that I was as screwed up as I was. Had I done so, I know damn well that they would have done anything to support me. But I felt that I didn't deserve that. I didn't deserve anything because I should have been happy and I wasn't. I also felt that I'd failed my parents badly and having destroying all that they'd done for me, I had neither the courage nor the heart to let them know what was really going on. I suppose too, if I'm honest, I was scared that my mum and dad would see me as an attention seeker. And that was the last thing that I wanted because everyone hated attention seekers.

The associated implications of attending a psychiatric hospital, literally a stone's throw away from college, were also too daunting to be entertained. Nobody in York knew me well enough to know that I wasn't insane. I had no way of judging what people would think of me and since I had little confidence as it was, had I agreed to attend the day hospital at that point in time, I seriously doubt that I'd have been able to face anyone from college again.

The consultant tried to convince me that the day hospital would offer me the greatest chance of overcoming my anorexia, but as much as I wanted to recover I felt too unsure of myself to agree to go. Instead, and very much as a last option, it was decided that I should continue seeing Dr Underwood on a monthly basis. In between visits I'd be expected to keep a 'food diary' in which I had to record everything that I ate and drank, noting my mood and feelings at the time. If I made myself sick or used laxatives, I'd have to record that too and I had to promise to take the anti-depressants regardless of whether I felt they were having any effect or not. Additionally I'd have to report once a fortnight to Dr Markham to be weighed.

As I left the consulting room having spent two hours at the hospital that morning, I felt mentally exhausted and totally drained. Had the full extent of my problems been unknown to me beforehand, now they were no more. Shedding dim light on what seemed to be an ever diminishing chance of recovery, the complexity of my anorexia was now more than clear to me and I knew exactly where I stood. I knew too that by turning down the suggested treatment, I alone was hindering all future progress. I deeply regretted not being of stronger character and resented myself for taking the easy way out. Not quite sure of what I'd expected from my appointment that day, had I hoped for inspiration I left with none. Viewing my situation to be pretty much hopeless, I was far from convinced that I'd ever defeat my anorexia. It was a beautiful spring like morning and yet as I walked across the car park to where I'd left my car, blinded by tears I was completely unaware of the world around me.

Still not happy about taking anti-depressants, when I next saw Dr Markham I voiced my worries to him. Furiously hoping to distract him into forgetting to weigh me, I also mentioned that since I'd been taking them my face had taken to flushing quite severely and quite often. He assured me that the drug I'd been prescribed was one of the safer anti-depressants, and explained that flushing was a common side effect associated with many anti-depressants, but suggested that I mention my face to Dr Underwood if the flushing persisted. Having gone to the surgery specifically to be weighed, needless to say, my stalling did not result in me escaping the dreaded scales. I didn't dare to look at the reading.

Embarrassed that I could not be trusted to look after myself without constant checking, I also felt saddened that I should waste other people's time through ridiculous self-neglect. That said however, at a time when I distanced myself from the care of family and friends, receiving and accepting care from the medical profession instead had become immensely important to me. I believed out of some perverse notion that my illogical behaviour and irrationality might puzzle those of far greater intelligence than myself, and so in my own peculiar world, provoking medical curiosity allowed me to feel different and I suppose even special. And I needed to feel special. The more I isolated myself from those who loved me, the greater the need became.

Medicine had always fascinated me and although I felt nervous about returning to see Dr Underwood, the prospect of gaining further insight into the world of psychiatry intrigued me. It had taken me a while to convince myself that seeing a psychiatrist did not automatically mean that I was mad, but I felt confident enough in myself to leave any psychiatrist in no doubt that I was not stupid. That was my intention anyway until fate chose timely to intervene.

The evening before my second meeting with Dr Underwood, I was involved in a drama exercise at college, and along with my contemporaries I was required to dress all in black and to colour my hands and face red. With limited resources and no grease paint, to achieve the desired red effect some bright spark mixed tins of crimson powder paint with baby lotion, whilst the rest of us slapped it on quite happily. In preventing the paint from cracking and in being kind to our skins, the baby lotion was deemed a great success. The contrast with the black was made and if I remember correctly the entire evening went well – until we tried to get the paint off. To my horror (along with everyone else's) I discovered that in sinking into my skin, the baby lotion had taken the powder paint with it. It was convincingly unshiftable, and whereas perhaps normally I'd have found it amusing to have crimson paint stuck all over my face, given that I was due the next morning to discuss with my psychiatrist the fact that his anti-depressants were causing my face to glow bright red, I didn't want to believe what was happening.

Seriously concerned that Dr Underwood would consider this evidence enough to believe me mad, I scrubbed at my face for hours with a nail brush until, along with the top layer of skin, I finally managed to get rid of the offending pigment. Sitting with my hands a little pink and my face still smarting from the night before, I found myself counting the flowers on the wall paper once again as I waited for Dr Underwood to open his door. When he called me through to his office, again I was subjected to intense questioning and again I left feeling drained. Requiring much thought on my part, whilst Dr Underwood tried to uncover vast areas of my past, I found many of his questions extremely difficult to answer. Concerned that I genuinely could not identify feelings and emotions that I felt I should have been able to identify, it worried me that I could recall relatively little of my childhood. I felt that the past and I had separated, and suddenly I realised that I had no idea who I had been as a child. I'd also lost the ability to interpret what I was experiencing here and now. I didn't know how I felt about being a woman, I couldn't identify what I really enjoyed doing, I didn't know whether I had sexual feelings or not, I couldn't remember ever feeling angry, and I had no idea about what I wanted for my future. I knew that I felt fat and that I was too frightened to eat properly, but beyond that I felt as though I knew nothing and my ignorance scared me.

In losing track frequently of what was being said I found myself unable to concentrate and without concentration I felt as though I was going nowhere. Feeling ill equipped to deal with the degree of stimulation that Dr Underwood's questioning technique bestowed upon me, my inability to come up with sensible, constructive answers to questions embarrassed me, gave me reason to doubt my intelligence, and caused me to believe that I would make little progress in talking to a psychiatrist alone.

By May, after two further sessions with Dr Underwood, I felt so desperate about feeling that I was beyond help that one evening, intent on harming myself in some way, I almost handed myself into the police because I feared not being able to control my actions. By coincidence the next morning I had my usual fortnightly weighing appointment with Dr Markham, which gave me an opportunity to talk. I rambled on for what seemed like ages without really knowing what I was saying; nothing made sense anymore and I felt beyond caring. Concerned that I wasn't getting the support that I needed, Dr Markham asked how I was getting on at the hospital, pondered over my doubts and asked me to return to see him a couple of days later. His whole approach had been so gentle and so kind that I'd wanted to cry. His genuine concern stayed with me and, having shared how I was feeling, as I left his surgery I felt calmer and more in control.

That evening, having come to the conclusion that I was not likely to benefit any more from seeing Dr Underwood, I decided to use any further sessions with him to gain insight into the workings of hospital psychiatry. And so instead of looking towards my next hospital appointment as one which would reinforce my 'stuckness', I viewed it rather as a way of satisfying my medical curiosities. I still felt hopeless; however, in having something of genuine interest to look forward to, I also felt happier. Consequently, when I returned to see Dr Markham my mood had lifted significantly and I felt a lot stronger than I had done.

As the end of my first year of college approached, in choosing housing arrangements for the following year, I made two significant realisations that helped me to bridge the distance that I'd created between myself and everyone else at college. Firstly, I realised that whether I liked it or not, I had some very good friends in York. Secondly, in suddenly noticing all around me people who really seemed to like and want to live with me, I woke up to the fact that whilst others had been prepared to make an effort to get to know me, I'd done my best to avoid becoming close to anyone. Realising that I'd grown afraid of depending upon people who I couldn't guarantee would be around forever, I also realised just how selfish my behaviour had become. I was determined to snap out of my unsociable ways, and amid the excitement of house hunting I lowered my barriers – having chosen to live with Ci and Caroline, I chose also to tell them and another friend, Gail, about my anorexia. Breaking my silence and with it my reluctance to make good friends, immediately I felt happier and more relaxed about living in York.

I spent the remaining three weeks of my first year at college, on teaching practice in a Doncaster middle school, getting to know Mary, my partner in classroom chaos. Together we worked hard and together we counted off the days until the last one of term. Three days prior to Mary and I leaving the school, I took the Wednesday off in order to return once more to see Dr Underwood. Thinking it wise not to inform the school (or my college supervisors) that I kept regular appointments with a psychiatrist, I chose instead to explain my absence with the well-worn but more believable, stomach bug excuse. Feeling guilty about lying and enjoying the morning in bed, I felt even guiltier for actually looking forward to what had become my monthly fix of attention.

Having already decided to confront Dr Underwood with my reservations about progress under his form of treatment, I found much to my relief that he shared my doubts. Making reference to both my food diary (see pages 66 - 68 for a typical 24 hour entry at that time) and the complexity of my anorexia, he willingly accepted that I needed more support than he himself could offer me. Given my particular needs, he concluded that I was left with no option other than to attend the day hospital as had been recommended in the first place. Words I did not want to hear, as in being more sceptical than ever, I remained unconvinced that day hospital treatment could do anything for me and once more I felt beyond help. I felt bitter that the system had failed me and impatient that I was too pathetic to sort myself out. I also felt incredibly guilty that I'd wasted Dr Underwood's time. But worse than that, by refusing to go to the day hospital and in rejecting the one option that he obviously held great faith in, I felt as though I was rejecting everything that he'd done for me and he didn't deserve that.

Compelled to eradicate some of the frustration that my stubbornness was creating, I offered to attend the day hospital on a part-time basis but was told that that would not be possible. After thinking for a minute, Dr Underwood finally volunteered that the only other thing I could try was counselling. I didn't believe for one minute that counselling would solve my problems but I was desperate to come away with anything other than nothing. I agreed to give it a go and arrangements were made for me to begin weekly sessions when I returned to college after the summer break. Leaving Dr Underwood's office for the last time, I knew that I'd miss the little things about him that had always made me smile. Watching his face as I replied to yet another question with an answer that probably made him wish he'd never asked it had never ceased to amuse me. Now I felt almost sad that I'd not be seeing my psychiatrist again. In the six months that I'd been meeting and talking to him, I'd covered little ground but had greatly appreciated knowing that someone had at least been trying to understand me. Dr Underwood had been incredibly patient with me. At times, I'd been downright awkward.

I was weirdly euphoric at returning home with the entire summer stretched out before me, but reality was all too quick to catch up with me. Having gone one sunny afternoon to my Stockton GP to ask for a repeat prescription of anti-depressants, when he asked me how I'd been getting on since he'd last seen me, I realised that my difficulties had actually worsened quite considerably. If it was possible, I was even more obsessed with food than I had been.

FOOD INTAKE RECORD

Name: Clare Lindsay   **Day:** Wednesday   **Date:** 8th March '89

Instructions: Please record everything you eat during a day. In column **1** record time food is eaten. In column **2** state the place, eg. kitchen, car etc. In column **3** state exactly what food or drinks you have had. In column **4** place a tick if you regard what you have eaten as a binge. Place a tick in column **5** if you vomited after eating. Also tick column **6** if you took laxatives. In column **7** briefly record you thoughts and feelings experienced before and after eating.

1 Time	2 Place	3 Food & Liquid Consumed	4 B	5 V	6 L	(Cals)	7 Thoughts and Feelings
2.30pm	College	Can D. Coke, black coffee, D. Coke.				- 400	Starving but ate too much yesterday to warrant eating before swim. Water freezing today. Burnt off extra 10-20 cals as result. Hated it today. Stomach still feels huge. Stomach is huge.
3.30pm	College	Porridge oats (raw, pinch), ½ kitkat, ½ cup low cal soup.				20 55 18	Wasn't going to eat until 4pm but couldn't wait, then couldn't stop. Want to eat all the time. Am scared I'll binge out of control again.
4.20pm	College	Can D. Coke, coffee, hot orange (low cal), ½ kitkat.				3 55	Craving liquorice – also soap. Got a bit in my mouth & now have taste for it. ?Mineral deficiency. Don't care. Freezing. 1hr 10mins to salad time.
5.40pm	College	College salad (ie. 2 pieces lettuce, ¼ tomato, 3 bits cucumber, cress), cabbage, coffee, D. Coke.			20	40 60	Serving lady always lets me have veg. with salad. I think she suspects something. Don't care.
6.22pm	College	½ apple, ½ kitkat, hot orange, D. Coke, D. Coke.				25 55 3	Freezing. Hands blue. Can't be bothered to shake them back into being pink. Chilblains hurt whether blue or not. Feeling fat, fingers puffy. Face awful. Pissed off with self for eating after 6pm when had decided I wouldn't. No will power, I'm crap. Don't want to exercise but will have to now, won't sleep otherwise.

1 Time	2 Place	3 Food & Liquid Consumed	4 B	5 V	6 L	(Cals)	7 Thoughts and Feelings
7.35pm	College	8 raisins, spoonful dry milk, coffee, ½ kitkat, ½ hot choc (low cal).				24 15 55 20	Boredom. Paranoia, what am I doing here?
11.46pm	College	Coffee, coffee, D. Coke, hot orange.				3	Pissed off. Didn't want to spend tonight with others but felt I had to be involved. Bored stupid all night, hated it. Wish I could get more time to self without everyone talking behind my back. Hate this place sometimes. All times! I just want to eat and eat and eat. Won't let self. Knackered, shoulders ache, bum raw. Feel so unfit. Wish I was fit enough to do more exercise, might not feel so fat then. Want to burn off everything I eat. Got to. No choice, too fat.
00.28am	College	550 sit ups.			20	-100	
01.15am	College	Today walked 80mins				-150	
Totals			0	0	40	-199	

My desire to lose weight had heightened and I was now making myself sick and abusing laxatives after almost everything that I ate. Hovering around six and a half stone I was finding it harder and harder to lose the weight that I needed to lose in order to settle my mind, and not a day passed when I didn't hate myself for failing – again. At night I was crying myself to sleep more often than not, and during the day I was living a nightmare. My Diet Coke drinking had got well out of hand, as had my need for exercise. I couldn't keep warm, I couldn't stop crying and I couldn't stand being away from Roger and my friends anymore. Crazed by food from morning until night and often in my dreams too, more and more frequently I encountered days when I couldn't face getting up. At times I didn't dare walk anywhere alone, scared that if I did I might jump in front of a bus, and often I thought I was going mad – genuinely mad. And all the time I felt so guilty.

Echoing only a catalogue of desperate attempts at recovery, sinister thoughts and memories told me that I was crap and I felt useless. Still stuck, I'd grown weary of unrewarded efforts, progress hadn't been forthcoming and life had become my greatest failing. Viewing hope very much in the same light as Carla Lane had once depicted in an episode of Butterflies, I too saw 'hope running towards the horizon with its arse on fire.' An horizon which constantly kept moving, tormenting me in the distance.

For almost one third of my life I'd lived beneath the shadow of my anorexia. Needing to break free from the vicious confines of my own body, with insight I'd come to understand how the powers of my mind and the pathetic burnt-out creature that I'd become, symbiotically fed one another – yet painfully starved me. For years I'd tried to separate the creature from the illogical behaviour. Unsympathetically, time had passed me by and month after month, along with those closest to me, I'd been denied peace of mind. I'd borne my anorexia as patiently as I could but now, with patience wearing thin, I was tiring fast.

Looking towards October I could see a final set of hurdles ahead of me. With only counselling left to try I feared running out of steam, but even more I feared running out of time.

Counselling

I'd been back at college a week before I attended my first counselling session, organised under the care of the day hospital. I met my counsellor, Katie, an occupational therapist at the hospital, on October 18th, 1989. Thereafter we met each Wednesday for an hour in the afternoon. During her initial assessment of me, as Dr Underwood had done before her, Katie scribbled down my history as I saw it at that time and together we then concentrated upon what I viewed my problems to be.

An expert at feeling fat, hating calories and craving food, identifying my difficulties came to me easily, as it would anyone with an eating disorder. Quite simply, I thought my difficulties were actually one. Or at least they all stemmed from one. Food. It was food that determined my size and weight and gave me reason to hate myself; and it was food that dominated my life, dictating every waking hour, stealing personality and excitement – rendering me crazy. I craved food never-endingly. I hated it. I blamed it for my depression and quite naturally I saw it as the very root of my anorexia. Yes. Food and my relationship towards it, were definitely the cause of all else.

Katie, I was quickly to learn, didn't share my views. For a start, she didn't seem to believe that my difficulties did stem from food and my relationship with it. Nor, as I'd automatically assumed, did she seem to believe that my depressed state had necessarily arisen as a result of my anorexia. And whereas for years, I'd been convinced that my disordered eating reflected solely a problem about eating, Katie, it seemed, wasn't. Doubting my logic, instead she appeared to view my anorexia as just one symptom of a much larger problem. A problem, or indeed a number of problems as yet uncovered, which she explained I would need to identify before further progress could be made. Shifting the emphasis of initial discussions away from issues centring only around food and weight, at first I found it strange that Katie should appear to favour discussing things which had nothing to do with my anorexia. Working with me she explained that in order to sort my eating difficulties out, I'd need to identify what was going on beneath them. To do that, essentially I'd need to develop personal awareness and I'd need to analyse and begin to understand the destructiveness of my ways.

Starting from a point of having virtually no awareness of either myself or my feelings, I spent my first session with Katie trying basically to establish a clear picture of what was actually going on for me. Guiding me away from fears and thoughts linked directly to my eating pattern, Katie encouraged me to forget my anorexia for a while and to think instead of everything else in my life that I was presently unhappy with. Having never really considered anything besides my anorexia as being problematic in my life before, at first I found great difficulty in identifying *anything* that I didn't blame upon my eating. Given time however, in addition to my eating difficulties I eventually managed to list seven other areas of my life which, in creating considerable anxiety and stress, also caused me difficulties. Independent of my fears around eating, I identified that:

- I had lost all sense of confidence
- I viewed myself as a total failure
- I had no direction or aims for the future
- I experienced a lot of anxiety around sexual feelings
- I felt helpless and hopeless
- I had low self-esteem
- I hated life and could see no point to it anymore

Although I didn't realise it at the time, by breaking my overall 'stuckness' down into what now seemed to be eight component problems, effectively what I'd done was place my anorexia into perspective. Now I could see it quite simply as just one part of a much larger problem. Working with Katie, once I'd established the importance of this learning, I then spent a considerable amount of time exploring how and why each of the eight smaller problems fed into and affected the others. Drawing all observations, realisations and links together on paper, Katie and I eventually created a much clearer picture of how I'd come to view and indeed experience life.

With each of the smaller problems feeding into low self-esteem, finally I could see what Katie had probably suspected all along. The central focus of my difficulties was low self-esteem, not my anorexia. But despite the fact that I myself had come up with the information concerned, I remained unconvinced that this reasoning could possibly be accurate. How could it be? If low self-esteem (and not my eating) really was responsible for generating and perpetuating my difficulties, why had I been oblivious to such a significant observation for so long? And why, if this really was the case and I'd had extremely low self-esteem probably for years, had I only been aware of problems created by my anorexia?

When finally I did allow myself to accept that my eating disorder was perhaps not the root of my 'stuckness', I made an important realisation. In the same way that helplessness and hopelessness, anxiety, loss of confidence, hatred of self and life, and feelings of failure, were symptoms of, and indeed a means of expressing, low self-esteem – so too was my anorexia. In fact, not only was my disordered eating an expression of difficulties associated with low self-esteem, so successful had it been at grabbing my thoughts and blocking all else from my mind, I could see now that my anorexia had become a coping mechanism. A mechanism of subconscious avoidance which had been for years, and still was, allowing me to struggle by by providing my mind with a means for ignoring issues and situations, feelings and thoughts, that I'd grown too weak to deal with.

So my anorexia had a purpose and I'd developed it for a reason. Feeling in some way that I'd made a huge breakthrough, for the first time I felt as though I was beginning to understand much of what had been going on. Before me I could sense that there was a hell of a lot to sort out but at last with Katie I felt as though I was getting somewhere.

I found talking in depth to a complete stranger a little odd to begin with. However once I'd settled into the routine of seeing Katie on a regular basis, I began looking forward to my sessions with her. Typically, once we'd dealt with the happenings of the week before, we'd then move on to work in depth with a particular issue or area of my life. With Katie the onus was always upon me to decide and assert what I wanted to work with and always I felt that it was my responsibility to try to help myself. Only when I appeared stuck would she offer any kind of suggestion as to what I might perhaps look at or think about next.

By being honest, both with myself and with Katie, I found myself recognising and uncovering feelings and emotions that for as long as I could remember, effectively I'd lost. Helping me to gain insight into the complicated world of my self-esteem, Katie encouraged me to confront fears and thought processes that had, perhaps for most of my life, been dominating my existence. By getting to the bottom of my low self-esteem and by changing the behaviours and thought processes creating it, Katie seemed to believe that my anorexia might well rectify itself. It would take considerable effort on my part and I would need to fully commit myself to learning about how and why I needed to change, but if I worked hard enough, I was encouraged that there was no reason why it couldn't be possible.

Raising both hopes and doubts, as hopeful as Katie was that I could learn to defeat my anorexia, I remained just as doubtful. I couldn't believe that the solution to my problems could be as simple as it sounded. Nor did I know whether I'd have the ability (or indeed the courage) to set about changing my behaviour and self to the extent that would probably be necessary, but I was determined to try.

Having established that my anorexia had arisen as a coping mechanism, I spent the first few months of counselling trying slowly to identify why exactly I'd needed to develop it. Beginning with the 'here and now', as I started to examine my present thoughts, perceptions and resulting behaviours, I found myself beginning to understand more and more about what was going on behind my anorexia.

Why can't people just leave me alone and let me do what I want to do? I've had enough of doing what everyone else wants all the time and I'm sick of it. I'm sick of being taken for granted and used like some sad dogsbody too. Why when people want something do they have to always come to me? I'm fed up with other people's demands. My time, my space, my things, my car, me – why does everyone want from me? Can't any of them look after themselves? I wish they'd just sod off and use someone else. 'Can I borrow this, have you got that, come and do this, will you give me a lift…' Leave me alone. Piss off and ask someone else. Can't people see how miserable they're making me?

I hate this, I feel like I'm being used all the time and I can't do anything to stop it. Trapped. Why can't I do what I want to do? Why can't I just be left alone? Time. I hate it. Every minute of the day I'm expected to entertain and occupy other people; satisfying them that I'm having a good time, when I'm not. Pretence, that's all it is and it's doing nothing for me but doing my head in. False smiles and forced me. Why can't people entertain themselves, why do they need my time, my space, ME? Why can't they leave me alone and stop using me as a doormat. Doormat, a bloody doormat that's all I am. Trodden on and walked over as though sometimes I'm not even there. Otherwise useless. Crap, worthless and utterly useless. A helpless no-hoper. God, I dread to think what people must think of me. Demands, demands and bloody demands, why can't I stop what's going on? Why can't I get on with my life like everyone else? All I want is to be able to do what I want occasionally but that's not possible. Nothing's possible for me. Why do I feel so guilty? Why do I have to do things I hate – all the time? Nobody understands. They'd think I was selfish if I said what I think and want, and no one would want to do anything that I wanted anyway. I'm too boring, no one could be interested in my ideas so what's the point? Being boring scares me. But I can't help it, I don't know how to be interesting. I'm so bloody crap, I hate being me. All I do all day long is just go along with everyone else, keeping them happy and me out of gossip. I'm at the end of my tether but what can I do – nothing, I'm useless. All I want is an easy life. Anything for one. Ha, that's a joke.

October 23rd, 1989

The first major issue that I worked upon during counselling was the overwhelming sense of powerlessness that had never left me. Causing me endless frustration (as my diary at the time reflected) as I began talking through those situations in which I felt powerless, the full extent of my ineffectiveness began to hit me. Feeding into almost any situation involving someone else, my inability to influence situations and people so as to ensure a happy outcome for myself, was a well-rooted one. Secured constantly by feelings of guilt and low self-esteem, my need to satisfy and keep others happy at my expense, was as much a part of me as the anorexia. More likely than not it was probably causing me just as much harm. Opening me up to exploitation and feelings of taken-for-granted-dogsbodyness, my inability to justify choosing or doing anything for myself was, according to Katie, just one feature of a 'predominantly passive behaviour pattern'. So too was my constant pleasing, my inability to make decisions and the 'shoulds' and 'should nots' which determined much of my behaviour. Forcing me to live a self-neglected life influenced by paranoia and fear, the passivity that controlled me was far from healthy. Lying at the heart of my low self-esteem, it was also something that I needed to understand more fully.

Helping me towards this understanding, Katie concentrated upon just one aspect of my passivity. Picking up on my 'need to please' she encouraged me to look at why I'd developed this behaviour by examining what I was gaining from it. Although I was not aware that I was getting anything from constantly pleasing other people, the more I thought about it the more I realised that I was. As far back as I could remember, I'd been gaining rewards from behaving well and satisfying those around me. Taking but a few examples: At school in the playground, my perfect friendliness ensured that my peers had no reason to bully or dislike me. In class, where I never did anything wrong, top marks and constant helpfulness secured me the attention I craved from teachers, which I didn't get otherwise from misbehaving or finding work difficult. And at home I gained peace of mind from believing that if I did everything possible to ensure that my mum and dad were happy, that might be reason enough for them both to love me.

Working in depth to uncover the full extent of my passivity, by the end of my third session with Katie I had a pretty clear idea of what exactly I was getting from always being passive. In striving for perfection in terms of treating others well, I was seeking (and sometimes receiving) approval, attention and affection. But what I couldn't understand was why I'd developed behaviours to secure needs such as these when I had no reason to want them. I didn't need approval, attention or affection. To seek any of these things was fundamentally wrong. To even think for one minute that I was selfishly trying to grab any of them for myself, left me feeling bad to the core and extremely uncomfortable. So uncomfortable in fact that before I returned for my next counselling session, I'd decided that if asked, I'd conveniently 'forget' what we'd discussed earlier and opt to talk about something else.

As it happened, when Katie and I next met I didn't have to think at all about what I wanted to discuss. There was only one thing on my mind.

Go on, boost my confidence

Am I an alien?
Do I have three heads?
Am I cruel and nasty?
Have I done something to hurt you?
Do I make you feel sick?
Am I repulsive to look at?
Maybe I smell.
Do I smell?
Or is it that I'm not worth bothering with?
Do you think that I can't think?
Or that I have no feelings?
Maybe it's me.
Yes. Maybe I'm the one who's aggressive,
    maybe I'm the pain in the arse.
I have no morals let's face it and I'm the one that's malicious,
    and my moods change like the wind.
No wonder.
No wonder you dislike me, and who could blame you?
Yes, I am an alien, I am three headed and faced,
    and I'm so cruel and nasty – I care for no one else.
And need you ask whether I'm aggressive?
No wonder you hate me.
I can see now why you try to hurt me. I'm vulnerable,

I'm down and I'm exposed,
And you need someone to kick don't you?
It makes me so happy to satisfy your needs,
* but you don't know that do you?*
No wonder you can't bring yourself to talk with me.
Again, I do apologise.

October 28th, 1989

Having spent much of the previous week wanting to be dead, when I next saw Katie I desperately needed to talk to someone. The fourth member of the house that I shared with Ci and Caroline had for weeks been treating me abysmally. Ignoring me, sniggering at me and refusing for no apparent reason to either look at or talk to me, Selma was hardly the friendliest person I'd come across and her behaviour had started to unnerve me. Calculatingly cruel, when Ci and Caroline weren't about she'd either yell at me aggressively or give me the silent treatment, broken only with snide stares and unspoken threats. When Caroline and Ci were around things weren't quite so bad, but still Selma was never pleasant to me.

Desperate for some reason to buy Ci and Caroline's favour, straight away I'd worked out that the sickening attention and gifts she bestowed upon the two of them (always in front of me), were just a ploy to win their friendship. At least that's what I thought was going on to begin with. It didn't occur to me that Selma might actually be trying to turn my house mates, and possibly everyone else at college, against me. To my rational mind at first that seemed ludicrous. As the weeks passed however and Selma's treatment of me worsened, I began doubting my own judgement of the situation. Selma was disturbingly nice to everybody except me, and I couldn't for the life of me work out what I must have done for her to turn so deliberately against me, but there must have been a reason.

I was being worn down sufficiently into really beginning to believe that I was evil, bad and despised. As Ci and Caroline received more and more gifts and I became visibly more hated, I moved beyond the realms of being able to rationalise the 'sad actions of a sad person' and began to really lose it. Paranoid and scared stupid that I was in some way to blame for the crap way in which Selma was treating me, it was a lousy bunch of flowers, given to Ci and Caroline amidst whispers and right in front of me, that finally brought me to breaking point. Either the girl was seriously warped or I was so despised that other people could only bring themselves to be awful to me. Regardless of which was true, I couldn't win. If Selma was as malicious as I sometimes suspected, she could quite feasibly turn people against me. If I was the one at fault, then her efforts wouldn't be needed. Everyone would grow to hate me anyway. Any faith I'd had in myself had been squashed and any hopes I'd had of remaining on good terms with my peers, crushed. What was the point? Efforts I made to smile and be happy and pleasant and everything else, would just be thwarted and no one would care and no one would want to know.

Desperate and lonely, I didn't know what to do. My head was fighting with itself and was of no use when it came to thinking. I was being pushed closer and closer to some kind of end; I needed to talk to someone but felt there was no one in York left to trust. I had to decide what to do alone. Torn between conflicting urges which told me over and over again to end my world and then to not, it was up to me. I could give in and stop thinking or fight and continue breathing. Guilt or paranoia: the choice was mine. Neither option was acceptable to me. As much as I felt too crap and useless to cope with life anymore, without self-esteem and strength of character, I was too gutless to shoulder the responsibility of leaving those behind me the legacy of my failings. Besides, I might have wanted death more than anything but I didn't deserve it. I was weak and too much of a failure. Suicide was too good an option. I'd done nothing to warrant the release it would give me. If my life was miserable it was my own fault. I'd made my own bed by not ensuring that I was happy and for that failing alone I deserved everything that I got. If I wasn't brave enough to make one decision – one simple decision – I deserved to suffer the consequences.

Bottling up and blocking out everything to do with the flowers episode, I managed to cope with what it threw at me only by eating nothing at all until I next saw Katie. Feeling faint and even weaker still, when I did see Katie and told her what I perceived had been happening to me, the depth of my feelings scared me. Allowing me just to talk and talk, once I'd exhausted myself and off-loaded everything to do with Selma, Katie encouraged me to think logically about *why* her behaviour was having the effect upon me that it was. Thinking in terms of my own behaviour, rationally I could see that the person who had caused me most harm during the last few weeks had actually been me.

Someone else might have been treating me as though I was the lowest life form on earth, but *I* was the one who had allowed myself to feel, believe and be affected by it all. Creating paranoia and desperately low self-esteem, I'd been the one who'd lost trust in my own opinions and judgement. I was the one when things had turned nasty, who'd automatically assumed blame and allowed the doubts to take hold. It was me that had failed to question the motives and indeed the sanity of the house mate's behaviour which had threatened to destroy me. And it was me who had negated positive self-qualities and personal rights, and lost feelings of worth, self-respect and decent innocence along the way. No one else had taken any of these from me. Only I could be responsible for losing them.

Likewise, I alone was responsible for the destructive cycle that carried me from self-doubts and non-stop pleasing, to perfectionism and the constant striving for standards which were too high and which ended always in failure, powerlessness and the self-doubts which kicked me round and round again. And I was the one whose behaviour had allowed and not stopped the downward spiralling that had almost broken me. The hurt and upset that I'd carried since the flowers episode had arisen because of me. Me and my ineffectiveness. I was the reason why Selma's behaviour had taken effect, and I was the one who'd allowed the situation to get as out of hand as it had.

Giving me a strange sense of control and almost power, when I recognised that I'd been responsible for the negative outcome I'd experienced, I realised that if I'd chosen to, *I* could have influenced things differently. Had I known how to stand up for myself and had I felt that doing so could be justified, with hindsight I could see that my position had actually been a strong one – until my behaviour weakened it.

Having now got myself into a rut it was up to me to get myself out of it. Unconvinced that I'd ever manage to improve anything myself, I began nevertheless to explore with Katie possible ways of ending what presently I couldn't cope with. To alleviate the immediate stress from the paranoia and fears that were still with me, I decided to trust my instincts and to tell someone else what was going on. I needed to know whether my perceptions of the situation were accurate and that I wasn't imagining things to be worse than they were. I also needed to feel that someone else was on my side and that I wasn't totally alone. Of everyone that I knew in York, Gail I decided would be the best person for me to talk to. A good friend to both myself and Ci and Caroline, Gail knew each of us well, was distanced enough to give me an outside-of-the-house opinion on things, and I could trust her. Not the type of person to suffer fools or unfairness gladly, she also knew Selma.

Feeling somehow less hopeless than I had done two minutes previously, having decided upon something positive that I was going to do, immediately I felt better. Knowing exactly what I needed to do, I also felt more confident. With Katie I'd worked out what I wanted to achieve from talking with Gail, I'd planned what I was going to say and I'd chosen when I was going to say it. Feeling that I was now in control, when I left Katie that afternoon I felt stronger and more empowered than I had done in years. To my further amazement when I spoke to Gail later that evening, within seconds I felt even better.

Offering herself immediately as a personal bodyguard and protector, Gail was brilliant. Quashing my doubts, she told me that not only had she noticed and been upset by what had been going on, but that Caroline and Ci had too. Each of them had turned individually to Gail before me, expressing their concerns over what they perceived had been happening in the house. Interestingly, Gail told me that I wasn't the only one who had a problem with Selma. Together and yet alone, for differing reasons Ci, Caroline and myself had each found ourselves bothered by her behaviour. Whilst I was being hated, Caroline had been plagued by never ending suffocation and Ci had come to believe that she too was being ignored. I hadn't been the only one thinking that I was going mad, nor was I the only one who hadn't dared to speak up. Not one of us had known where we stood with Selma. It hadn't just been me. Maybe I wasn't as mad as I thought I was.

Alerting me to the destructiveness of my own and other people's behaviour in the absence of effective communication, Selma and her flowers had taught me a lot. Bringing me to my senses and achieving the opposite of what had been intended, together they had brought Gail, Ci, Caroline and I closer. Securing for each of us greater trust, understanding and friendship, Selma and her weirdness were a threat no more and I for one felt happier.

That dealt with, for a few days I felt as though I could deal with anything.

God I'm disgusting, I've done it again. How did I let myself do it AGAIN? Why didn't I stop? Hell I've eaten loads. Bloody hell I don't know how... HOW MUCH HAVE I JUST EATEN? I didn't stop. Why've I done this, why didn't I stop? Shit, I hate this, I absolutely hate it. Why am I so crap? Why can't I control anything? Will I ever control anything? I deserve this. I deserve to feel fat. I've just bloody stuffed my face for God's sake – what else can I feel? – I'll have to get rid of it. How much did I eat? Why don't I know? How will I know when I've brought it all back up, whether I've got rid of it all? I can't do it. How can I get rid of it all when I don't know how much I've stuffed down myself? Stupid cow, I deserve this. My stomach's huge. I can't stand it. I want to rip at it and rip at it and rip at it, tear it inside out – get everything out. I didn't need to eat and I did. I can't believe I've done it again, God how much have I eaten? I'm going to have to be sick, but I still won't be able to rest. I might not get rid of it all. I won't be able to eat anything more all day. I'm just huge and disgusting – again, again. I don't deserve to get out of this, I deserve everything I get – I'm stupid, bloody stupid and I'm out of control. I've got to get this food out of me now, all of it NOW. I can't stand it a minute more. I won't let it make me fatter. I won't...

November 22nd, 1989

I'd lost count of the number of times that I'd stumbled out of bed to make myself sick, only to find on reaching the loo that there was nothing to bring up and that I'd dreamt another binge that hadn't happened. As I progressed with counselling, I became aware that my thoughts and fears around food always heightened when I uncovered difficult or painful issues. When the blocking action of my food-obsessed thoughts reached my dreams, usually that was a good indicator that subconsciously I was trying to hide from something. Having explored and dealt with a number of issues stemming from my anorexia and the passivity that caused it, when I began to look at why I'd developed anorexia as a coping mechanism, I dreamt of nothing but food for weeks.

During the course of two counselling sessions in which Katie and I had looked in depth at my childhood, I'd unearthed a couple of home truths that had left me feeling vulnerable, extremely sad and very uncomfortable with myself. As privileged and as stable as my upbringing had been, slowly and painfully I'd come to realise that maybe I'd developed anorexia partly as a means for securing the high levels of love and attention that I thought I craved but couldn't possibly have needed. An admission that shamed me deeply, in thinking for one minute that I hadn't been satisfied with everything that my parents had given me, I felt so guilty that for weeks I couldn't see how it could possibly be true. But maybe it was. I loved my mum and dad dearly and I'd always felt incredibly proud to be their daughter. Yet for me to have grown up craving attention, surely that would suggest that, like everybody else, I too had needs that perhaps sometimes hadn't been met. But that didn't seem possible. At least it didn't until I thought about it.

Surrounded by messages and living examples which taught and reminded me constantly of how lucky I was compared to everyone else, nothing gave me a better feeling about my mum and dad than the knowledge that they did more to help needy kids and families than anyone else I knew. That said however, given that I found it scary at the best of times to think of myself before others, maybe the 'hyper awareness of other people's needs' that I'd developed at home hadn't been as healthy for me as I'd always believed. Having grown up perceiving that my needs were less important and less real than the 'genuine needs' belonging to others, whilst I never felt that I lost anything to the kids my parents helped, indirectly because of how I reacted, perhaps I did. Thinking back over my childhood, as my awareness of other people's neediness had grown, so too had the feelings of shame that I experienced if ever I wanted anything.

Finding it easier to negate rather than justify any needs I had for attention, maybe over the years I'd come to crave attention because I'd always sought to deny it. Given too that I'd also learnt to deliberately avoid doing anything to seek attention, maybe this was even more significant. Highlighting once again the now familiar pattern in my behaviour, whereby craving always followed attempts of denial and avoidance, this observation opened up a third possible explanation. Making a great deal of sense, maybe the cravings that I had for attention stemmed directly from my inability to recognise personal needs and my reluctance to ever ask for any to be met. Maybe these missing skills also created difficulties for me when it came to the issue of my wanting too much in terms of love. I don't know why when I felt that I had everything and I didn't doubt for one minute that my parents did love me, that I should want more – but I did. Maybe I wanted love because I felt unlovable. Maybe I craved it because I couldn't let myself believe that I was loved. Or maybe I was just expecting too much of everybody around me. I don't know. But if I'm honest, my wanting to feel loved was still there. In fact it wasn't so much a wanting: like my selfish need for attention, my need to feel that I was really loved was a craving too.

Of all the realisations that I made through counselling, the implications of the above two saddened me most. Casting doubts on my belief that I'd not wanted for anything during my childhood, if I'd developed anorexia in part response to unmet needs, that would suggest that the childhood I'd perceived as perfect had perhaps not been. Feeling disillusioned and almost betrayed that parts of my past didn't quite live up to the 'perfect little world' images I'd created for myself, in many ways I also felt lost. Leaving nothing but doubts and unknowns in its place, my perceived reality may well have been unhealthy and unrealistic, but at least it had existed. Shattered, now it didn't and I didn't know whether I'd ever be able to trust my mind again. Up until now everything within my childhood had been faultless. If I could no longer believe in what I always had, what could I believe in?

Demanding and then rejecting of attention and love, if things hadn't been how I'd perceived they had, God knows what sort of a bitch I'd been. Making me anything other than loveable, my behaviour could hardly have been fair to those around me. No wonder I'd sometimes felt unloved. How could anyone love me as much as I wanted when I made it impossible for them to do so? Not knowing what to think anymore, the one thing I didn't want to believe was that I maybe hadn't received the unrealistic amounts of love that I thought I had. This panicked me desperately into feeling that I'd been making unfeasible demands on everyone; I felt like the worst little girl in the world. Not liking what I'd realised about myself, for a while I wanted nothing more to do with reality. The truth hurt: my dreams told me that.

Suddenly I felt disillusioned and very upset, as though I didn't know who I was. Nothing around me had changed and yet everything had, and I didn't know what to make of it. Frightened that I was becoming lost in myself, I phoned Roger pretty late that evening. I wanted him to make sense of everything for me and to reassure me that everything had actually existed. I also wanted him to take from me the pain that I couldn't even explain. More than anything I just wanted to hear his voice and to know that he still cared. Crying before I even got through to him, when Roger picked his phone up and I did get to hear his voice, rather than calming me down as it did usually, for some reason tonight it upset me all the more. Too upset to talk, I didn't know why I couldn't stop crying but I couldn't. I couldn't hear anything of what Roger was saying either and that freaked me. The words he was using didn't make sense. I couldn't string them together or get any kind of meaning from any of them, and I certainly couldn't form any kind of reply. Too distraught almost to be bothered to continue holding the phone to my ears, as my money ran out and the line went dead, I felt nothing. Later I felt dreadful.

Totally unaware of anything other than the tears stinging my face, as usual I'd been too wrapped up in what was going on for me to think about anybody other than myself. I hadn't stopped for one minute to think about Roger. I'd been the one who was upset and had needed to call, but what about him? Sobbing at him when he came to the phone and sobbing as the last coin dropped, God knows what he must have been left thinking. I might have been the one crying but he was the one left 250 miles away, distraught at not knowing what was going on or where I was or what I might do. Too numb to even realise sometimes that I was breathing, time after time whenever the money had gone, I'd just go back to my room. There, protected from feeling, whether my tears dried or not I at least always knew that I was safe. Roger didn't. Frightened out of his wits and helpless to do anything, whenever we were apart Roger worried constantly about me. Never knowing what was going to happen next, in all the time we were parted he never had peace of mind. He probably seldom had that when we were together either, not that I would have noticed. For as long as Roger had known me I'd been anorexic and whether I was aware of it or not, just as the illness was destroying me, slowly it was destroying him too.

I was still selfishly zombiefied and refusing to think seriously about the effect of my illness on other people, particularly Roger, when I next met Katie. She encouraged me to look at how I handled personal responsibilities. Feeding back to me a number of observations, she told me that she'd noticed that I often didn't deal with responsibilities healthily. Whilst sometimes I avoided responsibilities that I should have taken on, I would take on others which I shouldn't have done. Highlighting the bigger of the two problems, Katie pointed out that every time I worried and felt bad (unjustifiably) about how someone else might be feeling, I was taking responsibility for feelings which weren't mine (and which weren't therefore my responsibility). Thinking about this carefully, I realised that I took responsibility for 'protecting' other people from negative feelings a great deal. I even took responsibility for other people's behaviour sometimes too.

A classic symptom of passivity and always at my own expense, I often altered or shaped my behaviour so as to avoid other people being upset or left feeling badly. Making sure that I never said anything which might hurt, anger or upset anybody else, whilst this inappropriate handling of responsibility denied other people my true feelings, it also cost me needs and respect which I couldn't afford to lose. My taking responsibility for feelings and behaviours which had nothing to do with me stemmed right back to my childhood when even as a tiny child I'd felt responsible for my parents' happiness. Aware whenever Gary or I misbehaved that our actions sometimes upset our parents and occasionally created friction between them, probably before I'd even started school, I was trying desperately to make sure that neither Gary or I did anything too wrong. Terrified that my parents might argue or fall out with one another if we did, whilst I interfered with my brother and bossed him into behaving how I felt we both should, ironically I caused myself nothing but trouble. Positively creating conflict between the four of us, whenever I tried to get Gary to behave as I felt he should, always I'd get told off for interfering and always my efforts backfired on me. Trying only to keep my parents happy and together (not that there was any real risk of them ever separating), I couldn't win. If I did nothing and Gary upset them in some way, then I felt guilty, bad and upset for them. If I stepped in and took responsibility for trying to protect their feelings, I upset them anyway by upsetting Gary. Whilst my intentions were always honourable, they secured me guaranteed hassle, and I don't think I ever benefited from them.

Recognising that it wasn't just at home that I took responsibility for other people's feelings and behaviours, I realised that my handling of responsibilities was something that I really needed to change. Weighing me down and draining me frequently of any energy for myself, I worried about and took responsibility for other people's feelings more often than I cared even to admit. If I walked down the street and saw someone homeless and hungry, I'd feel so bad about being me and not being able to end their crap circumstances, that my guilt would haunt me. Friends, family, neighbours – if anyone around me was having a hard time which I felt could have been prevented, I'd feel responsible and bad in some way for not having stopped whatever. Even people I'd never met before could have a profound effect upon me. And animals. Hell, if I saw a maltreated dog or an injured rabbit or any animal in pain, I'd take its thoughts and feelings and carry them round with me, sometimes for days.

Stealing experiences which weren't mine, feeling for others came to me more naturally than feeling for myself. Quite why I wasn't sure.

Always strong and apparently happy to take whatever I threw at him, Roger was perhaps the only person who I didn't feel overly responsible for. Leaving him very much to his own devices regarding his worries concerning me and my well-being, if anything, when it came to Roger I shirked responsibilities. Largely unaware of the effects that my anorexia was having upon him, when I should have accepted responsibility for feelings of fear, worry, frustration etc. that I caused him to experience, I didn't. Inexcusable and totally unfair, I took his strength and ability to cope for granted and I abused his refusal to give up on me. Not taking the time nor the care to step outside of what I was experiencing, maybe I'd grown too close to Roger to distinguish between his hurt and mine, my feelings and his. Whereas once mine would have been the only feelings and needs negated by me, maybe it made sense that I should ignore his too, now that we'd become as one and had gone through so much together.

But that wasn't fair and whether or not it was true, either way I had no excuse. Roger was the most precious thing to me and all I was doing was abusing him by securing my needs at his cost. Ashamed to think that I'd not been aware of what I'd been doing to him, I tried to convince myself that my behaviour hadn't been having an adverse effect upon him, but couldn't. Shocked into seeing things from Roger's point of view, as I tried to imagine what he'd been forced to put up with, all I could think of was him crying.

I don't think I'll ever forget the first time I saw Roger cry. He was the first man I saw break down in front of me and it was my fault. We were watching 'The Carpenter Story'. I hadn't wanted to watch it with anybody else but Roger wanted me to watch it with him. He probably wanted to make sure that I saw it. I think he thought that if I saw somebody else die from anorexia that that would wake me up to myself – but it didn't. The film didn't even touch me. Karen Carpenter died from doing to herself exactly what I was doing to myself, but so what? Yes it was sad that she died, but it was also reality. At least dead she was no longer suffering. Death was just one of those things, a way out perhaps. It wasn't something that upset me.

But that was where Roger and I differed. Whereas I was too caught up in self-neglect to realise and indeed care that I too was risking death, Roger either saw or thought it every day. He saw and knew too, the suffering I could no longer feel and slowly it was eating him away. Not that I could see what was happening to him. (My 'feeling fat' thoughts cushioned me all too well from pain and sadly that included pain belonging to others.) Of the two of us, I had the easiest time by far. Oblivious to almost everything, all I had to deal with was feeling fat. Roger had to deal with everything else. Yes I was the one with the illness but he was my senses. I encountered; he felt, suffered and coped with everything.

God what was I doing to him?

Sixteen. Seventeen. Ten minutes and twelve seconds gone – forty-nine, forty-eight to go. One sixth down, five sixths left. Fantastic. Nineteen. Twenty… Twenty-three. Two more and I'll be a quarter way through. Oh God I've still got seventy-seven to do. Seventy-six. Seventy-five. Seventy-four. This doesn't get any easier. I wish I could just get out. I can't, I've eaten too much. Only forty-five minutes to go. Forty-one. Forty-two. Nearly half way. Eight more lengths and that'll be 270 calories. Two hundred and seventy, that's more than a kitkat. If I keep going that's what I'll have when I get out. I wish I was out now. Sixty-seven. Sixty-eight. Nearly seventy. GET OUT OF MY WAY. Stupid man. Come near me again and I'll kick you. What do you think I'm doing this for – fun? Plonker. Sixty-nine. Less than thirty-five to go, I'm knackered, completely knackered and I want to get out. I hate swimming – eighty-two – I bloody hate it. Seventeen left. Ten minutes more, then I can get out. Four hundred and fifty calories gone, ninety to go. God the tiles on that wall are boring. They couldn't be more boring if they tried, all ten thousand five hundred and eighty-four of them. Boring, boring, boring, hell this life is worth while. Ninety-four. Ninety-five. Five left. That's right mate, you swim across the pool. Everyone else is managing to swim up and down, and no one else has crashed into me three times tonight but don't you worry about it. You just continue. We'll all avoid you. It's difficult isn't it, up and down rather than across? Prat. Bloody prat. Four lengths left, yes.

Three. Second last length. Last one. Eight strokes to go, seven, six, five. Yes I'm there. OK freezing changing room here I come... Right, home, aerobics, sit-ups and then bed. Twenty-three whole hours of no swimming, bliss.

I hated exercise but I was addicted to it. Swimming, jogging, running up and down stairs, aerobics, squash, mini trampolining, sit-ups, speed walking – if it had a name I was abusing it and despising every lousy minute of it. At home, daily I was jogging, bouncing on a rebounder, doing sit-ups and careering up and down the stairs for hours. Not allowing myself to stop until I'd completed the necessary distance or time or number of whatever, every day I burned myself to the bone and every day I despised my life even more. Loathed that I should 'have to' run from one end of the house up the stairs to the furthest point and down again to the furthest downstairs point, over 200 times a day, and that I should force myself to complete 500 sit-ups a night (on top of everything else), I didn't like exercise and I certainly didn't enjoy it. Like so many other things in my life however, as much as I hated exercise, I needed it to satisfy my mind that whatever I'd eaten had been more than dealt with. Whilst I despised myself for being too weak to give in to this particular addiction, my obsession with exercise had become a necessary evil and one from which I couldn't escape. Completely obsessed with depleting calories and filling time with 'worthwhile' activities, when I wasn't experiencing the pain of shattered limbs and a worn out body, I was living the dread of the next day's fix.

It was damaging and sometimes dangerous, and without doubt I was pushing myself far too hard and yet again I couldn't see it. Or if I could I wouldn't. As long as there was food on my mind and time on my hands, nothing could stop me from exercising. Aching from head to foot wasn't enough. If I could stand up and walk then I could run, and if I could run then I could fly up the stairs and jump up and down. If I couldn't do any of these then I could swim and whether I could or not, always I had to do my sit-ups. Even when I'd carpet burned most of the skin off my bum and had to place newspaper beneath me to stop the seeping warn away scabs from marking the floor, I had to do 500 of the bloody things.

Desperate to free my thoughts of guilt and my body of calories, I didn't realise quite how dangerous my exercising had become until the night I woke up in casualty not knowing how I'd got there or what was wrong. Having eaten only two fingers of kitkat all day and having given blood (and with it however many grams of protein) half an hour before swimming ninety-two lengths of the college pool, perhaps it wasn't surprising that I'd collapsed in the changing room immediately afterwards. Too light to give blood legitimately (I'd been stupid enough to hide the truth behind a huge jumper and massive lies about my weight), I was probably lucky not to have drowned. Not that this would have made any difference to anything. Waking up a drowned rat in a strange place had been embarrassing and it had scared me, but to be honest, had the opportunity existed the next day to give blood and swim, I'd have done the same again.

If the warped state of my mind that day gave any indication of the deepening level of despair that was encroaching upon me, it didn't hit home until a few weeks later.

On My Sodding Own

Why, why me? Why should I succumb to a disease that rips my inner self apart? Constantly it tests me, pushing me to limits it knows damn well I'll have to break. I hate this life, I hate this disease. Always it's with me – I can't hide from it and when I want to shut off, I can't – it won't let me. I'm not allowed. Bitch, life's a disaster and one from which I can't escape. All I want is to be normal and yet look at me. Look at me, I'm useless, pathetic, crap and hopeless.

Nobody can help me, I'm beyond all comprehension, and it stinks. Why can't someone do something – anything? Nothing could be worse than this – knowing that everything's up to me. I don't want it, I've had enough. Help. Why can't anybody help?

I'm so alone with this addiction. This fucking disorder is mine, it's part of me and it's all too clear that things won't change. Somebody do something.

Put me to sleep, put my mind to rest – anything. I don't care. I just don't care, I'm doomed.

Sod this life, sod my diseased mind. I'm pissed off. Can't anyone sodding understand that? Can't they see what this fucking illness is doing to me? Take it from me, please take it, someone please.

Please don't leave it up to me. I don't need to hear what you've got to say. I don't want to, I can't believe that I'm beyond help. But then you tell me that I am and that it's up to me.
I have the control yet I'm powerless.
On my own again.

April 4th, 1990

Frustrated that I was still anorexic and very depressed despite my efforts through counselling to change things, I felt so desperate one afternoon in the April of 1990 that I called in to see my GP. I wanted him to do something to make things easier for me. I wanted him to say something or to prescribe something that would take my feelings away and cure my disordered eating (without me putting on weight) *now*. I needed someone to take responsibility for me for a while. I'd struggled on and on and now I'd had enough. Counselling was most definitely helping me but it wasn't solving everything now, and I needed it to. But as much as I pleaded with Dr Markham to do something, he could do nothing. There wasn't anything that he hadn't said or tried already and we both knew it. I'd had it. Beyond medical intervention, by concluding gently: 'I'm sorry but I'm afraid it's all down to one person now', Dr Markham was telling me what I didn't want to hear. Nobody else could solve my problems for me. When it came to defeating my anorexia, only I could do anything about it. The responsibility was mine and no one else's. I was on my own well and truly.

Stuck and feeling helpless, when I next saw Katie I took my worries with me and together we tried to look for new ways in which I might help myself towards making the progress I needed. Reviewing the progress that I'd made through counselling I realised that during the six months I'd been working with her, I'd begun to appreciate not only *why* but perhaps also *how* many of my present difficulties had evolved.

In striving for perfection, I could see that my personal expectations had always been too high. And in having an impossible ideal image of the person that I wanted to be, I could see too why I'd come to fear and dislike the person that I'd become. Having not been intelligent enough to pursue medicine as a career and in genuinely not wanting to do anything else, I could understand why I held no hopes or aims for my future. In summing up all of these failings, I could justify why I'd come to perceive myself as useless and I could understand partly why I'd developed some of my forms of behaviour.

Lacking all confidence and feeling unworthy of anyone's attention, in admitting that I perceived the needs of others to be more important than mine, I could see how I'd come to neglect my own. Without doubt, my eating disorder and self-abusing ways had become a way of communicating needs and expressing feelings which verbally I denied. Painfully aware of the anguish and misery that 'feeling fat' brought, in living a life constantly disrupted by irrationality and fears, I'd grown desperately used to feeling helpless and depressed. And when I recognised finally, that the perspective with which I viewed my shape and size had extended to mask and distort every other aspect of my life, suddenly I could see too just how misguided my perception had become. Unable to either communicate or express myself effectively, I had become completely passive, completely unassertive. I could see why I'd reached a point of no longer being able to cope and I could now appreciate why my anorexia had become a necessary coping mechanism in my life.

Scared into passivity and mechanisms of avoidance, negative thinking and self-neglecting ways; that my self-esteem was low remained a mystery no more and now everything made sense. With Katie I'd reached a point of understanding. Understanding which had opened my eyes and triggered many realisations, and understanding which now brought me face to face with the beginnings of the active recovery, which for so long I had sought. And where all other methods of treatment had failed, by providing me with insight, awareness and understanding of myself, up to now counselling had benefited me enormously. Unfortunately as I was beginning to learn, for me, counselling on its own did not hold the full answer to my difficulties. No longer gaining as much from counselling as I had been, after a few sessions spent exploring why I'd come to a halt, together Katie and I realised that our sessions together would take me no further. Too deeply rooted to be corrected by theory and insight alone, as much as I detested my anorectic behaviour, it remained stubbornly part of me. I really was stuck.

Totally floored by the prospect of being back at square one, I found great difficulty in coming to terms with the fact that hope was deserting me once more. Without hope, I simply couldn't cope anymore. Convinced that I'd never recover from my anorexia, my 'stuckness' overwhelmed me. Having reached a level of despondency quite unmatched by that which I'd entered before, I spent the Easter break of my second year at college wanting so badly to have the responsibility of my illness lifted from my hands, that I deliberately tried to deplete my body of potassium in the hope of inducing a heart attack. When, despite much researched efforts, I came to no apparent harm, I could only conclude that my body had joined forces with my mind and turned against me too.

But potassium or no potassium, as much as I wanted the responsibility of my life taken from me, I had absolutely no right to even attempt to impose the responsibility of my welfare upon anybody else. I hated myself for even trying but without the intelligence that I needed to override my anorexia, of just two options left open to me, bringing about a 'natural' end to my life, for a while, had seemed most favourable.

Counselling had done a lot for me. But as much as I'd gained and as much as I'd learnt, I needed more than just counselling. I needed to experiment, practise and consolidate what I'd learned. I needed to gain confidence and self-esteem, and perhaps more than anything I needed to develop the coping skills that I so badly lacked. Attending the day hospital, otherwise known as St. Andrew's, was my last remaining option. Katie stressed to me that St. Andrew's would provide me with the best opportunity available to begin putting everything into practice and to begin making things come right. I didn't believe her. But with nothing else to try I had to admit that agreeing to go did at least make some sense. The consequences of effectively turning my life upside down in order to do so however, still terrified me and although I realised that I'd be crazy to turn down the only remaining source of help available to me, I wanted time to consider my decision. I returned home to Stockton in the June to discuss my plans with Roger and agreed to meet Katie at the beginning of September to inform her of my decision.

If 1990 was to be one of the hottest summers on record, for me it was also to be one of many doubts. Aware that really I had no option other than to attend the day hospital programme offered to me, it wasn't until the very end of August that I finally decided to give full-time therapy a try. I had no idea quite what I was about to let myself in for but, reassured by Roger and my friends, deep down I could sense that I was doing the right thing. Admitting to the psychological severity of my illness, and consequently taking a year out from college, I knew would come as a huge shock to almost everyone who knew me, especially my parents. But it was also something that I knew I had to do.

PART THREE

St. Andrew's Day Hospital

St. Andrew's, one of only two counselling and psychotherapy units in North Yorkshire, at any one time provided specialist treatment for up to twenty-one clients experiencing difficulties with psychological, emotional and relationship problems. Working within the framework of a structured timetable, the main aim of St. Andrew's and the therapy undertaken there, was to provide a safe environment within which clients could be encouraged to help themselves through difficulties. Incorporating both small and large group work together with individual counselling, the timetable positively encouraged quality group interaction and shared problem solving between group members (clients and staff), with the intention of promoting the development of self-awareness, personal skills and self-esteem in all clients.

Large group work, involving all clients and one or two members of staff, varied daily and as shown overleaf, included: Creative Activities (usually discussion based games); Projective Art Therapy (which did not, as I imagined, involve the hurling of great pots of paint at walls); Drama Therapy; Swimming and Water Polo; Relaxation and Stress Management; Awareness Sessions; and Group Beginning and Ending Meetings. With all clients expected to attend all large group activities, the resultant sense of community aimed to provide everyone with the ideal opportunity to develop trust within the group; to express themselves and to share feelings and difficulties; and to help one another not only to solve problems, but also to have fun.

Breaking up the large group activities for an hour each day, the large or whole group divided into three smaller *small groups,* each comprising up to seven clients and one or two therapists. Working confidentially in separate rooms with the same people each day, small group sessions provided a safe talking environment for clients to discuss personal issues. During small group sessions clients were encouraged to work upon specific individual issues, using the help and support of the rest of the group, to, for example, consider and explore possibilities involving risks or change. Varying constantly from day to day, the nature of the work undertaken during small group sessions depended at any particular time upon those issues the group members elected to discuss.

Timetable of Activities

Monday	Tuesday	Wednesday	Thursday	Friday
9.30–10.00	9.00–11.00	9.45–11.00	9.30–10.30	9.30–10.30
Week Beginning Meeting 10.00–11.00 Small Groups	Individual Counselling Sessions	Swimming and Water Polo	Relaxation and Stress Management	Small Groups
Break	Break	Break	Break	Break
11.30–12.30 Discussion Games	11.00–12.00 Small Groups	11.30–12.30 Small Groups	11.00–12.00 Small Groups	11.15–12.00 Week Ending Group
Lunch Break	Lunch Break	Lunch Break	Lunch Break	Lunch Break
1.30-3.30 Projective Art	1.30–3.30 Drama Therapy	Free Afternoon	1.30–3.30 Awareness Group	Free Afternoon

Often extremely intensive and perhaps the most essential component of St. Andrew's programme, small group work generated enormous group understanding, strength and support and this in turn encouraged clients to take risks which otherwise might not have seemed possible. Facilitating vital personal realisations and self-learning, small group work relied entirely upon client input and demanded a willingness to share and to respond to feelings.

In addition to group work, on a regular basis, each client received individual counselling sessions with a designated key therapist.

Responsible for the assessment and management of client progress throughout the treatment programme, the role of the key therapist was to assist the client in identifying a workable plan of action, from which progress could be both structured and directed. Working closely with the key therapist, typical individual counselling sessions would involve clients in trying to identify personal issues to be tackled; goals to be achieved; and strategies to be employed to facilitate positive behaviour changes.

Commencing and then drawing to a close each week of the St. Andrew's programme, every Monday morning and every Friday just before noon, time was set aside for everyone to meet together. The meetings provided clients and staff with the opportunity to express feelings and ideas. Each Monday, the week would begin with everyone announcing to the whole group a statement of intention for the week. And each Friday the week would close with everyone 'feeding back' to the group, not only progress that they themselves had made during the week but also any progress that they had observed in other people.

Settling Into Therapy

What is it, where is it and what will it be like? Will I like it or will I hate it? Will it like me or won't it? Will I like me, and what about everyone else? Will there be anyone else? Will anyone want to know me and what I'll be? What will I be? Will I fit in or will I fit out? Accepted or detested, an outcast or a freak, happy or sad? Lonely, will I be lonely and scared, and if I am will anyone care? What if no one does, what then? Then where will I be and what will I do? Is there any point in finding anywhere when there's no one there to care? No one. Is that what it'll be like, have I got it wrong or right? There's no way of knowing. Not until I get there. Scary, this place sounds scary and I have my doubts and no answers. There are no answers, there can be none and like death there'll be no going back either. Will I want to or will I want to stay? No one can tell me and I can't yet. Oh hell, what is it, where is it and what will it do to me – this place they call the unknown?

August 29th, 1990

It had been a long time since I'd last felt confident enough to be myself. So long in fact that had anybody suggested to me in the September of 1990 that I'd learn to defeat my anorexia within five months, I most certainly would not have believed them. I had no idea what the programme offered at St. Andrew's could do for me and I did not look forward to the prospect of spending months tied up in therapy. Having exhausted all other types of therapy before however, now I could at least see that really I had no choice other than to commit myself fully to the day hospital's programme. So on September 12th, feeling very much like a child about to attend school for the very first time, I arrived at St. Andrew's for my first full day. Clueless completely as to what to expect, walking up the drive I wished until my mind ached that at that particular moment I could be somewhere else. Anywhere would have done.

I was more scared than I'd been for a long time and I couldn't remember the last time I'd felt as apprehensive as I did. Dreading God knows what, I think I was more unsettled by not knowing what I'd find behind the doors of St. Andrew's, than St. Andrew's itself if that makes any sense. Never having seen anyone other than Katie when I'd called at the same building for my weekly counselling sessions, didn't help. Faceless, the people I was about to meet worried me. Who were they? What would they be like? Would they be mad? Did they really exist or was this all some mad bad conspiracy to trick me and grab control of my trust and understanding? Why had I never seen or heard any of these people before? Did they speak, could they move? And how many of them would there be? Would they like me or think me mad? Would I scare them, would they scare me? Basket cases. Would they be basket cases? Was I making a mistake? Did I know what I was getting into? Did I really want to come to this place – me? If I wanted to leave would they let me? Or would I have to escape and if I did would it be possible...

With my imagination running wild, as I entered the large sitting room I was taken aback to find the room filled with laughter. Katie leapt up from her seat to meet me and straight away she introduced me to the twenty or so people scattered around the room. Greeted by a host of smiles, instantly something about the place struck me. These people didn't look mad. They looked completely normal. Totally removed from an image that for some reason I had feared, St. Andrew's was nothing like the place that I had stereotypically perceived it would be. There was a definite warmth about the place, a feel of acceptance and a sense of fun. Jokes were flying freely across the room and yet these people, like me, were supposed to be depressed. Their faces should have been etched with sadness and hopelessness, their actions suicidal and strange, silent and awkward. And yet they weren't.

I'd feared that being in the company every day of other depressed people would bring me down. I'd also feared that everyone at St. Andrew's would be so different to me, that neither they nor I, would want anything to do with one another. I couldn't have been more wrong on both counts. Indistinguishable from the six members of staff dotted around the room, every client had a different story to tell. And yet, regardless of race, age, sex or background, incredibly perhaps we each had much in common. We shared a need for approval and a wanting to be liked; we shared unspoken empathy and mutual respect; we shared an ineffectiveness and a kind of self-loathing; but above all else, we shared a compulsive caring and immediately I found myself amongst friends. Within a week of joining St. Andrew's, I realised that my time spent there did not necessarily have to be traumatic.

Having previously worked in great depth with Katie (now my key therapist), I found the transition from once weekly counselling sessions to full-time group therapy far less daunting than I'd anticipated. In observing what was going on about me I sensed a unique richness of interaction unlike any that I'd experienced before – a 'specialness' that brought people together – and I noticed feelings of enhanced trust and understanding. I noticed too regardless of presenting problems, that where there was a personal willingness to tackle issues, at any time any client could call upon the rest of the group for help, fully assured that help would always be there. Surrounded by mystical unspoken philosophy, I found myself subconsciously absorbing feelings of self-worth and importance and I began to appreciate that I had the same right as everybody else to have personal needs met.

By the end of my first week at St. Andrew's, having previously resigned myself to believing that I'd remain anorexic and depressed for the rest of my natural days, I began to notice small changes in my thinking and I sensed within me that somewhere I had the ability to think differently about myself. Having started on the Monday by stating that my aim for the week was to settle in to the programme, within five days I'd accomplished my first goal. On the Tuesday Katie and I discussed a 'problem management plan', identified major issues that I needed to concentrate upon and drew up a weight contract, which was to ensure that my weight did not fall below seven stone whilst I was attending the day hospital. (As stated in the contract, if I did fall below this weight I would be asked to leave therapy.)

Feeling safe to experiment and to begin taking risks, as the end of my second week at St. Andrew's approached I was aware that my outlook on life was beginning to change. In an attempt to pin-point and appreciate what exactly was happening around me I began to record on paper the happenings of each day. In trying to capture the essence of my first few weeks in therapy, amongst many issues that had cropped up within that time, three in particular stood out as having had a significant positive effect upon both my thinking and my behaviour.

Firstly, in being accepted as a welcomed member of both the large group and my small group, I'd developed the confidence to begin taking small risks. As a result of doing so, regardless of the nature (or triviality) of the risk being taken I'd received enormous respect and support from those around me and I'd felt valued. I'd learnt too, that taking and conquering even tiny risks brought me feelings of achievement, and that that made me feel good.

Secondly, I found myself beginning to challenge my lack of decisiveness. With increasing awareness I was beginning to appreciate that when faced with a decision, it was *my* responsibility to choose an option that *I* wanted. Constantly surrounded by issues (both individual and collective to the whole group) arising from inadequate self-assertion, gradually I was beginning to understand that choosing options to keep other people happy, at my expense, was not my responsibility. Nor, if my needs went unmet as a result, was such behaviour fair or healthy. Slowly, in beginning to see myself responsible for having my own needs met, I began to recognise and acknowledge myself as an equal. Something that I'd never done before; another step forward in my thinking.

The third significant area of change that I'd noticed concerned my self-esteem. During the short time that I'd been attending the day hospital, with increasing self-confidence and feelings of worth, my self-esteem had rocketed. Chipping away at the negative attitude that I'd always held against myself, with increased self-esteem I found myself accepting compliments that previously I would have negated and I found that people genuinely seemed to accept me. I found too that by being completely honest in explaining to college friends why I'd taken the year out from my studies, nobody rejected me.

In fact, far from it. My friends, and indeed my entire year group, were totally supportive of me. When I told Ci and Caroline what I'd decided to do, I think they were both surprised but relieved. Really pleased that I'd decided to sort myself out, Caroline hugged me and told me how worried she'd been that something might happen to me. She admitted that she'd been scared every night that she'd wake up the next morning to find me not breathing in my bed. Worried that I'd been so depressed, Ci hugged me too and told me that she just wanted me to be happy. Echoing what I was to hear almost every time I met someone from my year, Ci wished me the very best and made me promise to come and find her if I wanted to talk or if I needed anything.

Accepting and genuinely interested in what I had to say, everybody from my course (except one) wished me well. Like Caroline and Ci, Nikki, Gail, Mary and Janet were particularly supportive and went to great lengths to make me feel that I was still part of everything at college. Inviting me to whatever was going on and meeting me regularly for coffees, their friendship and support boosted me enormously. So too did the concern and new, but genuine, attention, that I received from peers who previously I'd hardly even known. Met with kindness every time I ventured into college, the eighty or so people in my year couldn't have encouraged me more if they'd tried. Touched that everyone seemed to have something positive to say to me or about me, of all the things that were said, those that were least expected made me think the most. It brought a lot home to me, when Martin said for example: 'I admire you, I wouldn't have the guts to do what you're doing. I really respect you for that', and Mark: 'Good on you Clare – go for it. I hope it works out for you'. Taking on board the good wishes that everyone seemed to have for me, I felt far better liked than I'd ever imagined. I also felt respected and the more I thought about everyone's kindness, the more my self-esteem increased.

In liberating many of the negative thoughts from my mind, I'd learned that by taking risks and absorbing feelings of achievement, worth and self-importance, that I could enhance my self-esteem. And with enhanced self-esteem, in my mind at least, there was room for optimism. Reviewing my position with Katie, although undoubtedly it was clear that I had been making definite progress, in admitting that I'd chosen only to tackle small issues which I perceived to be relatively safe, I knew that I still had a long way to go. I needed to get to the bottom of my personal ineffectiveness, I needed to identify long lost feelings and above all, I needed to change my behaviour in more ways than I cared even to imagine. Discussing with Katie those areas of my life which I wished to be different, I didn't find it difficult to identify how, in theory, I wanted my life to change. In reality however, since I feared the unknown more than anything else, the prospect of personal change did not appeal to me and, aware that I'd find many of my desired goals extremely difficult to achieve, I seriously wondered whether any of them would be possible.

Climbing down from my September pedestal aware that I'd barely uncovered even the tip of the iceberg, I knew that, ahead of me, I had much to do. September had treated me gently. October, I realised would be different.

> 'October and the trees are stripped bare,
> Of all they wear, what do I care,
> October and kingdoms rise and kingdoms fall
> And you go on… and on…'

'October', U2

And so October arrived bringing with it both the trials of autumn and the imminent sense of uncertainty from which I could no longer run nor hide. Unsure of many things in my life, having never confronted the concept of change on a personal level before, I had no idea why I should feel threatened by it, but I did. Highly critical of the person that I perceived myself to be, and aware of numerous personality traits that I wished to eradicate, deep down I knew that I would benefit from changing my ways. And yet at the same time I could sense that something was holding me back.

Restricted by the belief that people had never had any reason to like me, for as long as I could remember I'd been living an act, choosing to display as nice a persona as was possible in preference to my own natural personality. In doing so I had rapidly dropped any 'real' sense of self and had effectively become a slave to the new founded 'niceness' that I'd desperately created. Hiding behind a false front, having surrendered the ability to stand up for what I wanted, I'd become somebody that nobody could ever really know. Capable only of pleasing others, the Clare that everyone else knew was a fraud. A weak pathetic feeble thing that couldn't handle criticism or awkward situations. An act which helped the true me avoid difficulties and emotions that I didn't want to face and which allowed me to strive for the social perfection that I longed. Not that I was perfect or anywhere near it and if anyone knew that, I did. Desperate to keep the majority of my horrors to myself, the not being perfect was what I really couldn't stand. It was also what I tried to hide most. And maybe I was convincing, I don't know. Too scared that people would become fed up with me if I moaned or admitted how I was really feeling, I didn't dare be unhappy. How could I be if I wanted my friends and family to like me? I had no right to be miserable anyway, or angry, or pissed off with anyone. That wasn't my job. My job, no matter how I was feeling was to be bright and cheerful and happy and smiley, always.

Had I at the time been aware of how deceptive my behaviour had become, that in itself would have greatly concerned me. However, having lost track of my true personality, I was largely oblivious to what was happening and I had neither the inclination nor the energy to begin questioning what I did not know was not normal behaviour. By ensuring that my name became synonymous with what I believed everyone else expected of me, whilst the false Clare in me attempted to satisfy my need to be liked by everyone, my natural personality weakened to such a degree that effectively I stopped being myself and lost all track of who I was or had ever been.

Although it was probably obvious to those who were trying to help me, I didn't actually realise that I'd alienated myself from myself until I forced myself one art session to confront my fears of personal change. Faced with the task of expressing artistically, on a piece of paper without words, what change meant to me, initially I could think of nothing to draw. After a while however, without conscious intervention I found myself scribbling, of all things, a pretty fluent picture of how I'd come to view myself. Given that my thought processes up until that point had appeared blocked or at best reluctant to deal with this particular issue, that I'd drawn anything was significant. That I'd apparently liberated part of my mind was even more so.

To the left-hand side of the paper I'd drawn a network of well-defined shapes differing in size and colour, each enclosed within a thick black line. Equally spaced to perfection, as if locked within the confines of a rigid pattern, each structure appeared isolated but safe, each attractive to the eye. Controlled by space and dominated by precision, as sure as appearances were deceiving, disharmony shone through and something seemed wrong. Echoing the imbalance of a strange mind, distinct from the first image, on the rest of the paper and using only black and grey I'd scribbled an image of chaos. Chaos which looked a mess and chaos within which nothing made sense. Completely undefined and lacking any kind of structure, aesthetically this image appeared unwantable. Unwantable and thrown down without care, only to be neglected and ignored by eyes of choice. Out of cruel disrespect, fearless black lines violated the grey and added spite and intolerance to the confusion. Filled with visual hatred, in screaming out 'avoid me' the message of the image was all too clear.

Analysing what I'd drawn I found before me two scary images which completely contradicted one another. In recognising that the first represented how I viewed myself at that point in time and seeing the second as how I believed I might be if I changed, I became aware of a number of things. For a start, I realised that I was deliberately not allowing myself to be myself and in seeing an image of what I did not want to be, I began to understand why. What's more, in sensing that I had much to hide, I realised that I was scared of finding my natural self for fear of what I might discover. Having little idea of who I really was, I could only imagine that change would uncover those parts of me that I wanted no one to know.

Now aware that I'd been putting on an act as a way of covering up what I felt to be the nastiness of my personality, I didn't know whether I'd be able to cope without it and I felt vulnerable. Additionally in fearing the worst, I really believed that change would exaggerate my many bad points and expose everything about me that others might justifiably dislike. Suddenly, by putting two and two together, it finally dawned on me that my fears weren't so much based around *change* as they were around *rejection*. It wasn't change in itself that terrified me. What I dreaded more than anything was becoming somebody that nobody else wanted.

A lonely word with an even lonelier meaning, rejection was probably the one thing that I was most scared of. Something I'd not really thought of before, I was so terrified of being rejected and not wanted that I'd not even dared think what it might mean to me. Knocked back into a sense of almost shame, strangely I felt guilty. Guilt, that for once I couldn't explain. Pulling me deeply inside myself and tearing me completely, I felt as though I'd done something terribly wrong and yet I didn't know what. Unsteady on my feet, I also felt sick. Shocked into realising that all along I'd feared rejection so badly that I'd not even dared admit to myself that that was what my real fear was, I didn't know what to think anymore. Now that I'd admitted that I was scared of being rejected, suddenly everything seemed ten times more real and ten times worse. No longer able to avoid either the word or its meaning, rejection no longer didn't exist in my life. Pulsing through my arteries and now my brain, very much alive and bringing feelings of failure with it; now it did. I had woken up to a truth I didn't want to face: I didn't want to know that I might be somebody that other people might choose to reject.

It had taken me a long time to make the link between the issues of change and rejection, and yet as soon as I'd made the connection between the two everything seemed so obvious. Stripped of the protection that my mental block had temporarily provided me, realistically I knew that I could avoid change no longer. More frightened than ever, just thinking about this brought nothing but terror to mind. As promised, October had given me a taste of what was to come and in wanting to hang on to my past whilst life charged on with incredible speed, I felt as the trees. Together we were powerless as to what was happening around us and together we felt threatened by the storms of autumn. Whipped by vulnerability and unsteady and insecure, standing still had long since become impossible and I realised that I needed to fight to get back my control. Scared sufficiently into pushing myself forward and determined not to fall, with hope, I knew that if I could survive the gales, in the spring I might rise again. With new insight and old intrepidity, I knew that if life was ever to seem worthwhile, I had to go on. I had to rise again.

It took a couple of days for the events of that particular art session to finally settle in my mind and certainly when they did they gave me much to think about. In getting to the root of my fears based around personal change, effectively I'd opened the door to greater progress and further risk taking. Resigned now into believing that I did have to change, I could sense how fast everything was beginning to move and I felt very uneasy. Barely confident that I was worth knowing as it was, I dreaded to think of what would happen if I did change.

What would it do to me? What would I be like? Who would I be? Would I still be me or would I become someone else? How would I behave? What would I say and do, and how would I know what to think? What sort of person would I become? Would I be a better person than I was now or worse? Worse in terms of being anyone, less wanted in terms of being a friend? Shit, what would people make of me? Would anyone like me? Could I ever like me? What if I couldn't and everyone else hated me too? What then? Would I be able to change back? Or would it be too late, the damage already done? And what of the past? What would happen to that? Would it still mean anything? Would I still mean anything? And in the future? Would I still think and believe the same things or would I become callous and uncaring? Could I still be passive and gentle or would I have to be awful and obnoxious? And what if I became angry and aggressive and impatient, or I lost my temper and couldn't control what I was thinking and everything I thought screamed out? What then? Who would like me if that happened? Could anybody. . . ?

With so many new ideas and doubts flying around my head, I couldn't appreciate what I was taking in and I was not in a position to think rationally. Determined to stay in control of my thoughts and aware that I needed to understand exactly what was happening as it happened, I began to systematically record those thought processes that I was aware of by scrawling down exactly what I was thinking (regardless of rationality) whenever possible. Basically I began to keep a much more detailed diary than ever before. As far back as I could remember I'd always kept a diary although never before had my writing actually served a purpose. Now however, in being something that I could consult on a regular basis, my diary had become a tool through which I could honestly express my emotions and channel my thoughts into some kind of constructive shape. It provided me with the daily opportunity to release those thoughts that I deemed too irrational to voice and, as such, in many ways it had became a personal confidante.

Looking back now, indirectly my writing perhaps helped me more than any other activity that I was involved with, although its potential value didn't actually strike me until late one evening whilst talking with a friend. Since I'd been in York, Dan had come to know my thoughts almost as well as I did myself, and as a friend I was sure that he would recognise the positive changes that I felt I'd already made. Having not seen him during the three weeks that I'd been at St. Andrew's, I phoned him and called in to see him. I wanted to share my progress with him but more than that I wanted to catch somebody else's reaction towards the whole thing. Worried about how I believed change would affect me, I also needed advice and reassurance that I could trust.

Armed with self-doubts, I wanted convincing that changing my ways would be a positive thing to do and I needed to know realistically what my goals should be. It was of paralysing importance to me that I knew in my own mind how people would react towards me if I did change and, although I did not want to, I had to find out whether Dan believed people would still like me or not. Trying to describe to him what I feared change would do to me, I remember telling him that I was scared that I'd hate myself. During the last few years my strange and bizarre ways of thinking had on many occasions baffled him and now was no exception. Dan had always maintained that he could not understand why I should doubt myself and that night, having started the evening by describing how well I'd been getting on at the day hospital, I could tell that the questions that I was now asking made even less sense than usual. Having tried many a time to convince him of how huge I was, now in trying to convince him likewise of how awful I was really, again my reasoning met confusion. As hard as I tried to demonstrate how selfish, uncaring and basically crap I was, he claimed that he couldn't see it.

Watching him that evening, I couldn't help but notice that from time to time a quick smile kept breaking across his face and I sensed that whereas once my thoughts had perhaps alarmed him, now they seemed almost to amuse him. I could tell too that he was probably thinking, 'my God, the girl is quite mad' type thoughts, which I suppose summed me up pretty well and also, in turn, amused me.

Who else in their right mind would choose to starve themselves? It was crazy. Nobody was forcing me not to eat and certainly no one was making me behave in the irrational ways that I did, and yet still I continued. Why? My life was a nightmare and here I was in control of my actions, striding full length from one ridiculous situation into another. If I wasn't starving, I was making myself sick. If I wasn't doing that I was stuffing my face with laxatives and living a lie. And then there was the exercise. The stupid running all over the house like a mad person, the swimming that bored me up the wall and the sit-ups that hurt so much I cried. What was I doing it all for? The choices I was making suddenly seemed so stupid and there was no doubt about it, they were just that. Nothing in my life made sense and yet I couldn't understand why I couldn't understand what was happening to me. But I didn't understand and all the time it scared the hell out of me. And yet I allowed the confusion to continue. Why? How could I be so stupid as to prescribe myself needless misery and restriction? I needed my head seeing to. I was having my head seen to! This was crazy. So ultimately crazy that to anybody else it was unbelievable and so unbelievable that it was almost funny. As a victim, I was letting life hate me. I was letting it look down on me and at every opportunity I was giving life full permission to laugh at my expense. And for years, circumstance had been getting away with it. This was seriously unfunny - or was it? Did life have to be so unfunny?

Suddenly I was beginning to see things differently. Certainly there was a very serious side to anorexia, but that didn't have to govern everything. For a few moments that night, I'd seen another side. Thinking precisely about the chaos that invariably surrounded the huge disaster area that I'd become, I realised that my life had become a true comedy of irrationality. Strikingly apparent now, it struck me as ironic that whilst all along I'd been living a life of pure ridicule, never had I interpreted any of my crazy ways as funny before. Having at last done so, I couldn't help but begin to view what was happening to me through a new perspective. A perspective that I could understand and one through which everything seemed less threatening.

Without question, that evening I learned a great deal. In facing up to the risk of asking someone to predict how they believed change would affect me, to a certain extent I'd tackled and indeed allayed some of my many fears around rejection. Dan's opinion had helped to settle my mind and effectively now, the prospect of personal change did not seem quite so daunting as it had until that point. Plucking up the courage to ask a question that I did not want to hear the answer to, had been an achievement in itself and I felt secretly proud of myself for having done it. Confronting head on one of my greatest fears – the facing of potential rejection – had turned feelings of self-doubt into feelings of confidence. And in realising that I'd substantially lessened the weight of the workload ahead of me, I felt more than a little pleased with myself. Additionally, in finally recognising the value of looking to see life from a new perspective, I was now also in the position of doing just that. Realising that I had the ability to turn everything around, I made up my mind to start laughing at life and myself, and I decided there and then never to let circumstance or experience get the better of me again.

But if this thinking was significant, it dominated my thoughts for all of two minutes before being totally over-shadowed by a crazy idea thrown at me by Dan just as I was about to leave. With a hugely wicked grin scrawled all over his face and in complete jest (I think), he remarked that my thoughts were so bizarre and so unbelievable that I should publish them. Appreciating the implication that I was an unknown entity, I laughed and thinking his cheek typical I probably kicked him for good measure. Knowing how mad I invariably was, throwing a crazy notion of any kind in my direction, especially in fun, was usually not a wise idea. Not only did the idea of publishing my thoughts amuse me and make me smile, it also registered as an idea that greatly appealed to me. I was also daft enough to give it serious thought.

'Why not?' I thought, with wild ideas about creating a book based upon my recovery from anorexia flying through my mind. Throughout my anorexia, I'd read as much literature on eating disorders as I could lay my hands on. Hard going as much of it had been, undoubtedly I'd gained vital insight which had clarified in the broadest sense, that yes, I had developed anorexia and that yes, it was my way of coping with difficulties in my life. I'd come to understand many of the numerous theories that depicted eating disorders as a response to society and social expectations, and I could see where I stood amidst it all, but *nothing* that I had read had convinced *me* that I would *ever* recover from my anorexia. I had insight, but no book had ever shown me *how* to make sense of my findings in order to achieve the personal answers that I needed.

Prior to me attending St. Andrew's, I'd been fully resigned into believing that I would never know a day free of anorexia and depression. Nothing that I'd ever read had given me enough hope to believe otherwise. Certainly there appeared to be a gap in the literature market. Without hope I'd come to realise that life was hell, sheer hell. If I could reflect upon my learning in order to provide hope and encouragement for others who, like me, desperately wanted to understand how to recover, then why not? If I could capture my experience accurately enough for it to be of some use to other people going through the same thing, that was something that I very much wanted to do. I wanted to prove to myself that anorexia was defeatable and if I could I wanted to provide an explanation of how recovery might come about. Of course in order for me to achieve any of the above, I would have to fully recover myself first. Obviously this created a fundamental problem. Far from losing sight however of the task that lay ahead of me, in my enthusiasm I saw this simply as a technical hitch in my plans to be overcome at the appropriate time.

Realising that I'd set myself a huge goal, I decided there and then to make writing this book a major part of my recovery and suddenly

I saw direction. That day, October 11th, 1990, I believe marked a true turning point. Certainly it gave me much to think about.

A Step-by-step Explanation of Recovery

St Andrew's Day Hospital: A day to day progress of the realisations, learning, and development of skills that enabled me to recover completely from both my anorexia and depression.

October 11th, 1990

> 'I feel so extraordinary,
> Something's got a hold on me.
> I get this feeling I'm in motion,
> A sudden sense of liberty.'

'True Faith', New Order

October 12th, 1990

Having gone to bed with my mind racing at the prospect of suddenly finding what I thought to be a unique answer to everything, today I awoke feeling indeed extraordinary. In the space of twelve hours my thinking had changed incredibly and I could hardly believe how positive I felt. Used to feeling completely crap about everything to do with me, for the first time in years I'd been able to look ahead and see something worth aiming for – and I couldn't deny that I felt good. And yet strangely that in itself felt bad. Stirring thoughts and ideas which threatened all that I believed, feeling good about myself could only be a bad thing. It had to be, surely? Positive 'self thoughts' could only be right if you were someone who deserved them, and I wasn't. Or was I? Did I deserve to feel good about myself? Certainly that was what I wanted. Thoughts or feelings? Which could I trust? Not knowing which of the two to stay with, feeling unusually strong and positive still, today I decided for once to throw caution to the wind.

As bad as I felt for admitting that I'd enjoyed feeling good about myself, I had enjoyed it and I didn't want to lose the thoughts that I'd had. Determined to hang on to my positive attitude for as long as I could, tonight I threw myself into planning ideas for my book.

October 16th, 1990

Still feeling positive and determined, I gained more from today's drama session than from any before it.

Concentrating upon developing group unity, the session was spent identifying and communicating positive qualities that group members saw in one another. Responding to questions such as 'Whose smile comes to your mind first?', 'Who would you most like to get to know better?' and 'Who have you noticed something different about this week?', throughout the session, we were each asked to think of the one person present who best fitted the criteria asked for. Having chosen someone, we were then asked to bridge a link between the question and person by placing and keeping a hand on their shoulder. Once the link had been made, we then had to explain why we'd chosen that particular person. With eighteen people in the group each choosing and identifying different people for different reasons, typically after each question the entire group would become tangled in the middle of the room, with linking arms literally holding everyone together.

It was an amazing exercise to be involved in, and I really enjoyed today. Receiving compliments from people telling me, for example, that they would feel most comfortable sitting with me if they wanted to be alone; that my sense of fun had cheered them up this week; or that my smile sprang first to mind because I'd been the first person to welcome them to St. Andrew's, surprised me and meant a great deal to me. The feeling of having been *chosen*, by others and in preference to others (an experience common to everyone in the group that session) was a lovely one.

Causing me to feel valued, noticed and appreciated, the session also forced me to think quite deeply, both about myself and what I'd just experienced. If people really wanted to get to know me better and to spend more time with me, because they felt comfortable in my presence or enjoyed talking with me, then perhaps I wasn't as undesirable and as worthless as I'd led myself to believe. On the contrary, perhaps for some reason people did genuinely like me. Having spent over an hour giving and receiving compliments I realised that, instead of instantly dismissing the good in favour of looking automatically for the bad, today I'd come away from the session taking with me the positive things that people had said to and about me. Allowing myself the luxury of believing and feeling good about the compliments I'd received, as if I'd succeeded at something I felt ten feet tall. I felt even guiltier than the other day for feeling that way but today I didn't care.

Jotting down those comments from the session that had had the greatest personal meaning for me, I decided to pay careful attention not to dismiss compliments in the future. Thinking too of the pleasure that complimenting other people had given me, I also decided that I'd begin to share complimentary thoughts more often instead of just keeping them to myself.

Having previously only seen drama sessions in a rather harrowing light, today, possibly because I'd felt more willing to join in than usual, I'd thoroughly enjoyed myself. I felt closer to everyone in the group and touched that so many of them should trust and feel close to me.

October 18th, 1990

Today was quite a mixed day for me which started off rather badly before ending unexpectedly well. Beginning with stress management which usually I enjoyed, today I encountered Tai Chi for the first time and absolutely hated it. Spending the first hour of any day deliberately concentrating on my body (the very subject of my worst dreams) whilst trying to discipline myself to move incredibly slowly, was not, I discovered, my idea of fun. As a form of relaxation, Tai Chi drove me to the point of distraction and left me feeling extremely frustrated. Aware that I was expected to participate in the session for its entire duration and feeling compelled to continue being involved against my will, I sensed myself becoming more and more wound up. And having chosen not to mention my thoughts about the session at the time – essentially because it simply did not occur to me to do so – I noticed that I remained on edge all morning. Feeling agitated and stroppy, although I wasn't aware that inside I was experiencing real anger, I took what I was feeling into the small group session and together my small group spent the whole hour pulling my feelings of anger to bits.

Having not connected how I was feeling with being angry, it wasn't until my behaviour was pointed out to me that I finally did make the connection. I couldn't remember the last time that I'd felt true anger and in realising that I simply hadn't recognised my feelings as those of anger, it became apparent to me just how out of touch I was with my emotions. I'd recognised that I felt frustrated but I couldn't understand why or how a harmless session of Tai Chi could have left me feeling as awful as it had done. Digging deeper with the help of the group, in pin-pointing exactly what had annoyed me I discovered that my anger had stemmed primarily from self-resentment, as a result of me forcing myself to continue doing something that I really did not want to do.

Furthermore, in looking at my behaviour in general I was quickly able to identify that this particular pattern was a well-rooted one. Having spent the vast majority of my life constantly trying to please other people by living up to the expectations that I perceived everyone had of me, often I did things against my will. Not recognising that my needs were not being met, typically as a result I'd feel taken for granted or hurt and upset and usually I'd feel worthless. Also I realised that in response to feeling unimportant, my self-esteem would dive and that as a result of that generally I would feel fat. Despite always swallowing my frustrations I never experienced feelings of anger. I only ever felt fat. Having started today innocently deceived into believing that for years I had managed to dissociate the destructive effects of anger from my life, I now had to accept that all along it had been very much part of me.

As far as I had been concerned, anger served no decent purpose in life. Because I'd always chosen to avoid it, I suppose I'd seldom encountered it at its worst first hand. I had, however, seen the effects of anger upon society and I had my own perception of what it could do. I associated anger with violence, hatred and regret. It damaged relationships, controlled lives, created fear, and since it left people feeling miserable in its wake, I wanted nothing to do with it. At best, I could neither understand nor entertain angry behaviour. At worst, it scared me to such an extent that I found it easier not to admit to myself that, like everyone else, it controlled me too.

My anger had gone unrecognised for a long time. For years I'd been biting my tongue, swallowing negative feelings and bottling everything up. The process had become automatic. Having developed a lifestyle that consumed anger and didn't let it go, I'd created a coping mechanism behind which I'd naïvely retreated from the pressures of everyday life. Unable to deal with situations effectively, instead of voicing my concerns, there was much I hadn't said and I had many regrets. I deeply resented the fact that food dominated my existence. I hated myself for not being able to control my life and with hindsight, now I realised that I was bloody angry. The most annoying thing for me was that I had no one to blame other than myself. At some point in my life I'd lost the ability to express myself effectively and I'd *chosen* to do that. No one else had forced me never to show my feelings or be angry. No, I'd learnt that for myself. It was my fault and if, as I now suspected, my avoidance of anger had something to do with the beginning of my downfall, that was my fault too.

Ignorance, personality weakness, cause or effect – idiot? The anger which had frustrated all known patience from me this morning was all my own doing and I blamed myself totally for the feelings of ill ease it had thrown at me – the result of years and years of neglected energy – which I should have been intelligent enough to recognise and at least detect. Wasted energy and wasted expression. Stupid. If I was bright enough to think myself into a depressed state where anger never touched me, I should have been clever enough to know that that wasn't healthy. I should have known how to override the thoughts which had damaged me and hell, I should have known not to bottle up my feelings. I should have looked for a way of expressing myself constructively and I damn well should have had enough about me to find one. But no, not me. Feeble and weak and stupid, I wasn't intelligent enough. Too thick, damn it, to do anything, I'd found no outlet for my anger. Scared of upsetting other people by saying or doing something I might regret, I'd learned to wimp out of anger-provoking situations. Too gutless to be honest with other people – or myself for God's sake – if ever anyone did hurt or upset me I kept my feelings to myself. Certainly I didn't let the offender know I was angry.

Useless and pathetic, whenever I failed to express my feelings when dealing with anger, I did the only thing I knew how. I turned it in on myself and I handled the consequences alone. Typically, whenever I did this I would do one of two things. My first response would always be to stop eating. Whether I did this to regain control or to torture my mind I honestly don't know, but the latter would always result. Almost as though I was trying to deliberately goad myself into feeling bad, I'd crave food until I could stand it no more. Whether my abstinence lasted an hour or a couple of days, always I'd get incredibly angry with myself for giving in, being weak and eating again, and always I'd feel fat.

Alternatively, and usually after I'd stopped eating, depending upon the depth of my anger, I'd work myself up into a frenzy and would deliberately attempt to hurt myself. And once I'd started I couldn't stop. Usually I'd fling my arm at the door, thrashing it and thrashing it against the door-frame until I could feel it no more. Although blackened and bruised, that was seldom enough. I wanted my arm to break. I wanted it to hurt and I wanted to hear it snap. But I could never do it. I wasn't strong enough even to inflict the pain that I deserved and that frustrated the hell out of me. I was completely powerless: my arms never relented and they never broke. But if I couldn't smash myself into release there were always other things I could do. Sometimes I'd stick pins into myself, more often I'd use them to rip skin. And then I'd tear at myself with my nails, breaking the skin deeper and pulling and pulling at it until whatever part of me resembled that part no more. Exhausted, bleeding and quite, quite black and blue, I never intended to seriously damage myself. I just couldn't help it.

Thinking about it logically, although it might seem hard to believe, taking my anger out on myself was actually quite useful. For a start it allowed me to deal with the full power of my feelings without having to worry about the consequences. What I did to myself didn't matter. It never involved anybody else, nobody but me ever got hurt and that was how I wanted it. As crazy as it might sound, I felt as though I was in control. I was in control. I was totally responsible for my actions, I knew what I was doing and it always worked. Physical pain dispersed my emotional feelings and by really letting myself have it, I'd experience a kind of release. A release which always brought eventual relief. The harder I hurt myself the 'better' I'd feel afterwards.

Additionally, and as much as I'm ashamed to admit it, causing myself true pain gave me an excuse to pay myself attention and I needed it. I needed to feel sorry for myself too, but that was something I could only do if I was in pain. With no reason to be depressed or angry, without hurting I couldn't justify feelings of self-pity. Being in pain lessened my guilt, and bumps and bruises provided me with visible signs of justification that all was not well. Born of frustration and a warped sense of logic, throbbing limbs were *mine*. They gave me permission to comfort myself and they gave me permission to cry. But when I did cry my tears weren't those of pain. More often they were simply the end product of a changing pattern of emotional expression. From a fearful starting point of powerful raw feelings, usually I would reach a point of mental and physical exhaustion. My body would ache and I'd feel extremely ashamed of what I'd just done, but my anger would be gone.

Throwing energy into self-harming behaviour from time to time gave me the release that I needed. It also very quickly became rooted within the self-punishing lifestyle that I'd both adopted and become addicted to. Regardless of how I dealt with anger however (although I'm pretty sure that no one else had any idea of what was going on) I seemed forever to be surrounded by feelings of guilt, shame and self-hatred. Certainly the shame that I felt drove me deeper into my secretive ways, and I always kept bruises, bumps and marks well covered.

Aware that I'd uncovered a huge area of my life that desperately needed attention, today I realised that if I was ever to repair the damage that years of avoidance had left behind, I'd have to work hard at getting back in touch with my true feelings – especially anger. Today's small group session had brought me to my senses and I'd learnt a hell of a lot about my behaviour. Together my fellow clients and I had identified where I'd been going wrong and together we'd shared our own and often similar experiences. I wasn't the only person in the group unaware of the effects that anger had played in our lives. Whether problems stemmed from non-recognition, lack of communication, misinterpretation or sheer avoidance; without exception we were all guilty of burying feelings and we were all living the costs of doing so. Discussing anger had very obviously touched a raw nerve within each of us and as a group we shared many unresolved issues related to it. We also shared mutual understanding and I for one felt reassured to know that I was not alone in not knowing how to deal with anger effectively.

Feeling that I'd made quite a significant breakthrough, I left today's small group session excited that I'd managed to identify something specific to work upon. I also left feeling a little scared. Aware that there was so much that I still needed to do, I couldn't see clearly how I could possibly mend all of my ways and even the thought of that frightened me. Feeling a lot calmer (despite my fears) than I had done this morning, as I drove home tonight I realised that as much as I'd hated it, I owed a lot to Tai Chi.

I felt confident that things were beginning to happen, and tonight whilst out with friends, a guy who hardly knew me from college tracked me down and gave me the following poem.

Don't Quit

When things go wrong as they sometimes will,
When the road you're trudging seems all uphill,
When the funds are low, and the debts are high,
And you want to smile, but you have to sigh,
When care is pressing you down a bit –
Rest if you must, but
don't you quit.

Success is failure turned inside out,
The silver twist of the clouds of doubt.
And you never can tell how close you are,
It may be near when it seems afar.
So, stick to the fight when you're hardest hit –
It's when things go wrong that
you mustn't quit.

Author Unknown

Beautiful words and a gesture so kind. That someone, *anyone*, should have thought about me in the way that Paul must have done touched me incredibly and boosted my confidence no end. I hardly even knew him, I'd done nothing to deserve his kindness and his gift had come completely out of the blue. Warming me and making me feel alive, it made me realise I had friends who I didn't even know were friends. People did care and that meant everything to me.

October 19th, 1990

Carrying on from yesterday's 'anger' session, as a focus for the week's awareness session, we chose to explore causal factors and behaviour reactions associated with all aspects of the emotion. In brainstorming situations which provoked me into feeling angry, I jotted down the following:

Not being able to get out of something I hate doing
e.g. Tai Chi.
Being asked to do something I don't want to do and feeling that I have no choice in the matter
e.g. being expected to go out when I'd rather stay in (resulting in me then feeling resentful all evening).
Feeling forced to volunteer to do something because I'd feel guilty if I didn't
e.g. offering friends lifts to the station to save them the cost of a taxi.
Being taken for granted
e.g. people expecting lifts because I have a car and I never say 'no'.
Feeling let down
e.g. when others aren't as considerate towards me as I am towards them, causing me to feel that no one bothers about me.
Being inconvenienced by others
e.g. not being able to watch what I want on the television because someone else is watching the other side.
Witnessing other people being taken for granted, or treated badly by others, and feeling both responsible for their hurt and angry with myself because I could do nothing to stop the situation.

Feeding back our individual lists to the rest of the group, I was amazed at how often similar situations to those that I had pin-pointed were echoed by other members of the group. Although everyone had their own pet hates, with striking familiarity I could identify exactly with almost every example given. Pulling prominent difficulties and examples together, as a group we were then asked to compile a list of issues common to us all. Analysing our findings, we found that, rather than certain situations being responsible for provoking feelings of anger, it was apparent that the root of our shared problems really lay within the way we each chose to deal with situations in general. As a group, I think without exception, we shared an inability to behave and communicate assertively.

More specifically, we shared an inability to:
> – value and acknowledge ourselves as equals
> – express our feelings
> – recognise our own needs
> – state our needs and ask for them to be met
> – acknowledge that we have the same rights as others
> – deal with expectations (perceived or real)
> – judge and deal with feelings of responsibility
> – deal with conflict
> – say 'no'

Seeing, written down in black and white, a collective representation of difficulties arising solely from lack of self-assertion, this morning it dawned on me just how unassertive I was. Having always mistaken assertive behaviour for aggressive behaviour, assertiveness had never been a quality that I'd tried to develop within myself. Now, however, in seeing assertive behaviour in its true light as an effective communicating tool, suddenly I saw a range of skills that I very much wanted to acquire. In order to become assertive (as defined by Stephanie Holland and Clare Ward in their book, *Assertiveness: A Practical Approach*, p.2, Winslow Press, 1990) I realised that I needed to develop:

– the ability to express ideas and feelings, both positive and negative, in an open, direct and honest manner
– the ability to stand up for my rights whilst respecting the rights of others
– the ability to take responsibility for myself and my actions without judging or blaming other people
– the ability to find a compromise where conflict exists

Realising that I possessed none of the above skills and recognising the significant contribution that each of them could make to my life, with painful reflection I could see where, for all of my life, I'd been going wrong. What I saw in myself, I saw also in the lives and experiences of those sitting around me, and I felt both sad and angry. If, as I now believed, my anorexia had developed because I'd never learned to assert myself and if, as it would now seem, my illness had dragged on for years purely because of continued ineffective communication – why had nobody ever told me?

How could it be possible for a child to spend twelve years in an education system, supposedly designed to prepare children for adult life, only to emerge as a young adult lacking in assertiveness skills so badly that he or she couldn't function at all? How and how could the omission of such fundamental learning ever be justified? As a teacher in training I couldn't help but feel that somewhere along the line, the education system of this country had let me down and I felt quite furious about the whole thing.

On a more positive note, if my eating disorder and accompanying depression really did stem from an inability to be assertive, it seemed logical to me to believe that the development of assertiveness skills could well set about reversing my anorectic condition. Having previously got to the point of identifying low self-esteem as the most probable cause of my anorexia, now I could see how, by never considering my own rights and equality and by never having asked for needs to be met, I'd neglected myself, lived for everyone other than me and allowed my self-esteem to slip. It hadn't just happened. My self-esteem had diminished for a reason. I'd been too passive for it to remain intact.

The more I thought about it the more this connection made sense.

Flawed

Covered bruises but no one knows
  the misery inflicted
    by a let-down system
  failed.
Someone should have seen it, someone should have cared
  but no.
Too valueless to communicate anything, when I said nothing
  you should have heard the false smiles
    and hungered excuses.

Shattered school day dreams and nothing much else
  a broken child
    with no respect.
Let down by intelligence makers who failed to see me
  failing, failed.

Pieces. Unhappy. Nothing.
Why didn't you notice that I'd fallen apart,
  that the pieces were cracked
    and I couldn't cope?
Couldn't you see that I couldn't function?
Couldn't you see that I needed to be taught?

Breakdown. Waiting to happen and perfectly visible, but hidden
  behind the uniform which covered but didn't excuse
    the lacking knowledge and functionless skills,
  of an education system
  flawed.

October 20th, 1990

October 22nd, 1990

Amazed at how often I fell into the trap of saying 'yes' to a request or demand when I should have said 'no', today I negotiated with my small group to spend the hour looking at ways of saying 'no'. Working as a group, once we'd brainstormed the pros and cons of being assertive and saying 'no', we then identified those difficulties and fears which most frequently removed the assertive option and led to us saying 'yes' against our wishes. Asked to then consider 'what happens when we do say no' and to compare our perceptions with 'what happens when we don't say no', we identified the following consequences.

As a result of saying 'No'

Negative Consequences

– we feel guilty
– we feel that we are letting someone down
– we fear hurting the feelings of others
– we feel that we are rejecting others
– we feel obliged
– we feel bad in ourselves

Positive Consequences

– we don't end up doing something undesirable
– we feel relieved
– we feel good about personal space
– we have more energy for desirable things
– we avoid feeling taken for granted
– we gain confidence

As a result of NOT saying 'No'

Negative Consequences

– we feel frustrated
– we feel angry
– we feel trapped
– we experience the doormat syndrome
– we feel used and manipulated
– we lose time for ourselves and our interests
– we lose touch with what we want or need ourselves
– we become stressed at work and/or at home
– we feel, or actually become, taken for granted
– we lose influence and confidence
– we feel weak and useless
– we lose ourselves to the demands of others
– we neglect ourselves
– we reject our own needs and health
– we lose self-respect and self-esteem

Positive Consequences

– we don't get repercussions from feeling guilty
– we avoid hurting other people's feelings
– we feel helpful, useful and involved
– we are less likely to feel selfish or unlikeable

Reflecting on the lists produced within the group, each of us could see quite clearly that saying 'no' was by far the healthier option for personal well-being. And yet I for one had great difficulty in accepting that saying 'no' was justifiable behaviour for me to take. How could I? How could I possibly justify putting myself before others, when all I'd ever known was that that was wrong? Yes OK, I could see that I had rights and needs, and yes I could accept that they were probably as important as anyone else's – but that didn't make everything all right. It still felt bad and I'd still feel guilty. Saying 'no' was perfectly OK for everyone else but not for me. If I said 'no' to something someone wanted me to do, that would be me being selfish. Surely.

I knew that wasn't the case really but my views on selfishness had been around a long time and they still scared the life out of me. Not that they ever got me anywhere. Realistically, I suppose, enough was enough. If I wanted to stop being anorexic I'd have to change. Being scared of being selfish had haunted and dominated my life for long enough. Sod it. If I wanted to become well again I'd have to become more assertive and if that meant temporarily going against my moral standings, then so be it. Sod my philosophy on life. Saying 'yes' and being passive might have been kind to everyone else, but it hadn't done me any favours and certainly I'd not gained any respect for it.

That said however, I still had to learn how to say 'no', and I still had no idea how to set about developing an effective technique that I could both use and live with. Voicing my lack of ease to the rest of the group I discovered that my concerns were universally shared and not unique. Katie suggested that it might be a good idea for us to look for strategies which would make the task of saying 'no' easier. Helping us to justify our thoughts and actions when saying 'no', she demonstrated how to turn down requests assertively and guided us towards producing the following:

Guide to saying 'No' painlessly

1) Clarify whether you want to do the request or not
Remember:
– initial gut response is a good indication.
– you have the right to choose what you want to do.

2) Believe in yourself and your self-worth
Remember:
– you have the right to say 'no'.

3) Buy yourself time to consider what you really want to do if you are unsure
e.g. say: 'I'm not sure what I'm doing tonight yet, I'll phone with a definite answer later.'

4) Accept that it is not your place to take on the responsibility of other people's feelings or actions
Remember:
– how a person chooses to react to a given situation is their responsibility. If they choose to react or behave unreasonably, it is *your* rights that are being neglected. You are not responsible, it is not your fault and you have no right to feel guilty.
– by saying 'no' you are not rejecting the person, you are rejecting the request. (There is a big difference).
– saying 'yes' (and then feeling angry or resentful) is not necessarily fair to the other person. They may be able to detect your feelings and may feel unfairly bad themselves as a result.

5) Own up to your feelings, share them with the other person and let them go
e.g. if you feel awful for letting someone down, say 'I feel awful for letting you down... but I don't want to...'
Remember:
– being honest is being fair (to self and others).
– people respect honesty.
– admitting to your feelings often provides a gentle starting point to rejecting a request and helps to prevent the other person feeling bad afterwards.
– departing negative feelings verbally is an effective way of releasing and letting them go.

6) Be honest and state your own needs to strengthen your case
e.g. state 'I don't want to go out tonight, I really need/want time to myself…'
Remember:
– expressing your needs promotes understanding and reinforces your equal importance to others.
7) Acknowledge the consequences of turning down a request by stating your appreciation of the other person's position
e.g. say 'I know that you were relying on me to baby sit, but I'm sorry, I really don't feel up to it tonight.'
8) Suggest an alternative arrangement to suit your needs
e.g. 'Perhaps you could ask someone else to baby sit for you tonight.'

As a major piece of learning, I knew that the implications of knowing how to say 'no' would prove invaluable to me. Feeling secretly confident that with time even I could master the art of asserting myself, I left today's small group session feeling strangely excited and determined to hang on to everything that I'd just absorbed.

October 23rd, 1990
For no apparent reason today I awoke feeling fat. Quite why overnight I should suddenly slip from feeling good back to feeling pretty awful, completely eluded me. It didn't make sense. I couldn't possibly have gained weight and actually become fat during the night, but I sure as hell felt as though I had. It wasn't even as if something had upset me emotionally to cause such a mood swing. But I definitely felt fat and I didn't like it. The only thing I could think of that might possibly have led to me feeling fat and depressed again was the good day that I'd had yesterday. Having taken on board a huge bit of learning, I couldn't help but wonder if this morning's fat attack had anything to do with my subconscious trying to slow me down by holding me back.

Still not sure, I described how I was feeling today at the beginning of the drama group. Asked if there was anything that I wanted from the group, without thinking I replied that I wanted attention and then feverishly wished I'd said nothing. What I should have said was that I wanted the group to know that I was feeling confused and sad, and that I'd appreciate everyone's support and perhaps encouragement. Instead, by stating that I wanted attention I was horrified at how selfish my demand must have sounded. The last thing I had wanted, or had intended, was to sound like a little spoilt brat but I had, and I felt incredibly guilty about it. Without an available hole to jump into, I tried to talk my way out of the mess that I felt I'd talked my way into and cringed throughout the entire session. Reassured afterwards that my statement had not been taken the wrong way by anyone, I felt less self-critical than I had done and decided to put the incident behind me. Like everyone else I was entitled to make mistakes and as far as I was concerned, this one would definitely be best forgotten.

I went to bed tonight feeling just as I had when I'd woken this morning. I didn't want to think about anything. I just wanted to sleep.

October 24th, 1990

Still embarrassed from yesterday's classic Clare clanger, I dived into the college pool that I'd abused thoroughly as a student and felt much better for abusing it again as a client of the hospital. Thrashing up and down an almost empty pool and then playing water polo, before relaxing in blissfully warm water, was my idea of hospital therapy. Messing about with the others and bringing terror to the waves, reminded me of my sixth form days and brought back many happy memories. Being small and pathetic, each Wednesday for a whole hour I'd tease carefully chosen members of the group (staff included) and as I always did with Roger and my friends at home, I'd get away with murder.

Tired but happy, today I drifted into the small group session secretly planning to continue my relaxed state by taking a nice quiet back seat for once. Katie, having watched me squirm the day before, had other ideas and suggested that I might benefit from exploring effective ways of asking for my needs to be met. Realising that I would indeed benefit from doing so, I postponed my bout of laziness and agreed to share and analyse my difficulties with the rest of the group. Again the difficulties that I expressed were not unique and again I found myself very easily identifying with the fellow feelings of unease, voiced by other members of the group. In much the same way that we'd tackled the issue of saying 'no', it was decided that we'd spend today's session initially identifying what it was that prevented us from comfortably asking for what we wanted, before then going on to look for strategies to overcome the problem. Those difficulties expressed by the group included:

- fear of being selfish
- fear of rejection
- difficulty in clarifying whether a request was reasonable or not
- doubting the right to ask
- feeling guilty about asking for needs to be met
- feeling too proud to ask, and stubborn attitudes
- thinking negatively, e.g. 'he/she wouldn't want/agree to do it anyway, so what's the point of asking?'
- inability to identify specific wants or needs
- fear of putting other people in an awkward position
- fear of request being misinterpreted and/or misunderstood (and didn't I know that one!)
- fear of embarrassing responses

From this starting point, having uncovered feelings and fears similar to those unearthed during the saying 'no' session, together we then identified the following assertive strategies to help eliminate perceived difficulties.

Asking for needs to be met

1) Acknowledge self-worth and accept that you deserve to have reasonable wants met
2) Accept that you have the right to ask
3) Imagine you haven't got the right to ask. Imagine you have. Which would you prefer?
4) Be sure of what exactly it is that you want
– Think before asking.
– Be honest with yourself, what would you really like?

5) Consider the needs of others, is your request reasonable?
– If yes, then go for it. If you have doubts, can the request be modified to make it reasonable?

6) State clearly and specifically what you want or need
Remember: owning and stating your feelings will help to justify your request.
e.g. If you feel really tired and you would like someone to help with the washing up, then simply say: 'I feel really tired tonight, please could you wash up.'

7) Remember that other people have the right to say 'no' too (without you taking offence)
– Accept that there will be things that others will not want to do.
– Remember that having a request turned down, does not mean that you are being rejected.
– Learning to accept knock-backs is an important part of assertive behaviour.

8) Think positively. (There are no guarantees but plucking up the courage to ask for what you want will increase the chance of your needs being met. You have nothing to lose, you can only win)

9) Do not feel that you are manipulating others
– How other people choose to respond (i.e. whether they choose to say 'yes' or 'no') is not your responsibility. As an equal, they have the right to assert what they want/don't want and it is their responsibility to do so.

10) Own your feelings and do not pass your responsibility for them onto others
e.g. If you feel upset/angry as a result of what someone else has/has not done, say: 'I feel upset/angry' instead of 'You have upset me/made me angry'.

11) Allow yourself to ask for help whenever you need or would like it

12) Regardless of the outcome, acknowledge that by asking for your needs to be met you have taken a risk. Think of this as an achievement and something to feel good about
Remember: Taking risks increases self-esteem.

Recognising that I now knew how to deal with issues assertively, at last I felt that everything was beginning to click into place. I still had to put my theory into practice, but life was slowly starting to make sense and I could tell that I was making real progress.

October 25th, 1990

This morning Katie told me during an individual review session, that I should think about leaving St. Andrew's towards the end of December. This implied that by then I should have developed sufficient skills to go out and face the world alone. I should have been happy, perhaps even delighted, to hear that I'd progressed so quickly, but I wasn't. I was horrified.

In the six weeks that I'd been attending St. Andrew's, yes, I'd gained confidence and self-esteem, yes I was learning to become assertive and had covered significant ground, and yes I could not dispute that Katie was probably right, but I didn't feel ready to leave. In fact I didn't want to and I didn't want to face the truth either. Feeling cared for and special on a daily basis had become an addictive component of my life. I'd grown used to the 'safeness' and the attention that being at St. Andrew's had given me and I didn't want to lose any of it. My thoughts were incredibly selfish. They were also an extension of my life and a part of me that I did not want to own up to. By admitting to myself that I was afraid of coping alone, I was admitting that perhaps for years I had *wanted* to be ill. Being anorexic had been safe for me and now, faced with leaving the safeness behind, I also faced the prospect of being well. In terms of coping with life, without my illness I'd be on my own. I'd have nothing to hide behind, I'd have no excuse for avoiding responsibility and I'd have to deal with problems like everybody else. Katie's words had destroyed my protective little world and suddenly I felt vulnerable and alone.

I didn't want to have to go back out into the big bad world. I'd had enough of it during the years I'd been ill to put me off it for a lifetime. I wanted protecting. I didn't want to have to take care of myself, I wanted other people to do that for me. They were capable, I wasn't. I was pathetic and feeble and all things useless. I wouldn't be able to cope and I didn't really want to anyway. I was quite happy where I was. St. Andrew's was doing me the world of good and I felt safe there. Safe and wanted. The world outside didn't want me. It didn't care. No one did. I'd be on my own again, struggling. Why did all good things have to come to an end? And why so soon? Too soon. Surely I didn't deserve to get kicked out yet. What would I do? How would I manage? Would I manage? Bloody hell, I'd just about managed to find my feet and now I was to be moved on again. What was the point? I might as well give up now. I'd been written off anyway.

Feeling badly done to and selfishly pissed off, I also felt angry with myself. In facing up to the changes that I'd achieved within myself I felt as though I'd tackled my problems almost too efficiently. Making faster progress than maybe I'd needed, if anyone had dealt me a future of looking after myself, it was me. I was the one who had cheated myself out of continued support. Perfect to the last, even in terms of securing recovery, I'd lost out. Typical, bloody typical.

Reflecting later on what had been said, today I found myself wanting to slip back into my old ways of thinking. It was a sad feeling to have and in many ways I dreaded December. Knowing that I now had limited time on my hands and that as yet I'd done little to kick my laxative addiction, tonight I realised that I could no longer hide from perhaps the most difficult issue of all.

My relationship with laxatives was not a pleasant one. For a start they stripped me of all independence and restricted my freedom. They tasted horrible and were expensive. They brought fear, shame, guilt and deception into my life. They caused me endless sleepless nights, when instead of sleeping I'd lie awake for hours writhing in agony. They gave me stomach cramps during the day, they dehydrated me and threatened to render me doubly incontinent. They had the potential to destroy my heart, my liver, my kidneys, my bowels. Hell, laxatives had the potential to kill me and yet I needed them. For two years I'd been taking up to twenty times the recommended dose of the most potent over-the-counter laxatives available, on a daily basis, and I couldn't recall the last time that I'd slept right through an undisrupted night. Nothing compared to the distress and fear that laxatives caused me and yet I couldn't bear to think of life without them.

Using laxatives was a coping hell. Nothing more and nothing less. They allowed me to justify a daily intake of 1,200 calories and they settled my mind that the consequences would be dealt with. Having endured years of eating between 300 and 600 calories a day, as much as laxatives were screwing me up, given the choice between returning to semi-starvation methods or continued laxative abuse, I knew which I preferred. Addicted to the peace of mind that eating more had given me, the prospect of resorting back to hunger-induced torturous thoughts depressed me incredibly. The thought of gaining weight terrified me and although I'd been fully aware that one day I would have to stop using laxatives, without them, now I feared being too scared to eat.

From day one at St. Andrew's, I'd deliberately pushed the issue of using laxatives as far from the vicious clutches of my mind as had been possible. Had I had to choose in September between a future consisting of 600 calories a day and a future consisting of nothing, hypothetically I would probably have chosen death as the most favourable option. It was now nearly November, I had only until December to confront my addiction and my feelings were still the same. Avoiding the issue of weaning myself from my habit had done me little good and now I realised that it was time to face the music.

Giving up laxatives would probably be the hardest single goal that I'd ever set myself to achieve. Aware that every cell in my body was most likely now dehydrated, I knew that in the initial rehydration stages (which would immediately follow my last dose of laxatives) I'd retain an enormous amount of fluid. And I couldn't even imagine what that would be like. I honestly didn't know whether I'd ever be able to give laxatives up but if I could, and I could find some way of achieving my goal without resorting back to starvation mode, then I'd be more than happy. With time running out, the prospect seemed an attractive one. It also seemed impossible. Nothing but sheer determination would get me through this one. Coming off laxatives would be up to me. I could run and hide or I could do something about it.

Feeling that the world was against me, tonight I was in too bad a mood to do anything other than be miserable. Thoughts of having to leave St. Andrew's had rendered me in a state of submissive self-pity. I was entitled to feel miserable and I was damn well going to wallow in it.

Totally knocked back, tonight in a bid to get back at the world I punished myself further and refused to eat anything until the next day.

October 27th, 1990

Invited to a friend's wedding, today I found myself wrapped up in somebody else's dream. Relaxed into enjoying what was going on around me, with a glimmer of hope I daydreamed myself into the future and tried to imagine my own wedding day. Dreaming myself into centre stage, I tried to picture myself soaking up the attention of everyone I had ever loved, attracted through pride and celebration rather than self-pity and self-neglect.

Thinking hard about my future, tonight I realised that I owed my parents and Roger a release from the shadows that my illness had cast upon them. I realised too that I owed myself the chance to enjoy life to the full again. I also had a book to finish.

October 29th, 1990

This morning I announced to the large group that my intention for the week was to search for strategies to help me overcome my laxative abuse. I didn't feel ready to give them up there and then, but by making a promise to the group to at least think about the problem I felt that I'd made a start.

October 30th, 1990

Today we learned that the girlfriend of a mutual acquaintance had been seriously injured in an accident, which had left her paralysed. I'd never met the girl involved but I'd grown to both like and respect her partner, and suddenly I cared enormously for him. I couldn't even begin to imagine what each of them were going through and I felt helpless. Helpless and guilty. Helpless because I was powerless to do anything that could possibly help and guilty because I had the audacity to allow my problems to be problems. I felt guilty too for abusing the many privileges that I'd always taken for granted, without stopping to think for one moment about other people. At any time I could choose to turn my back on my troubles and I could choose to walk away from everything. Physically for me that was perfectly possible. The very thing that some people could never do and hell I'd never given it a second thought before.

Shamed into viewing my position from a new perspective, tonight I felt compelled more than ever before to finally pull my selfish act together and to sort myself out for good.

November 1st, 1990

This morning in the small group session I was observed to switch off completely from what was going on around me. It was really strange. I could remember sensing friction and hostility between two members of the group at the beginning of the hour, and I could remember feeling uncomfortable because of the atmosphere but I couldn't remember anything more. In the seven weeks that I'd been at St. Andrew's, never before had I encountered conflict within my small group and never before had I been observed to visibly withdraw from the group, into my own little world.

Unaware of what had happened, my response had been subconscious and in my own opinion rather extreme. Surprised at the lengths that my mind had gone to to cushion me from the threat that I obviously perceived conflict to be, I realised that at some point I desperately needed to address my fears around conflict. Thinking about it logically, I suppose my lack of understanding concerning conflict made sense. I didn't like conflict and I never had done. As far as I was concerned, like anger, conflict served no decent purpose in life. All it did was generate fear. Threatening and controlling, to other people the term 'conflict' probably brought some kind of necessary meaning but to me it didn't.

To me, conflict meant Gary and I cowering in silence and darkness on the landing at home, not daring to listen but needing to hear every word being exchanged by our parents, mid row. Waiting for an end to the shouting, maybe because it only ever happened once or twice, I can still remember wanting and wanting the voices to make up, terrified that if they didn't it would mean divorce. Too scared almost to breathe, with shaking breaths and shivering bodies, my brother and I were too young to understand that sometimes arguments happen. An eight-year-old and a six-year-old, too frightened to believe that we weren't to blame, too green to know that raised voices and angry words didn't have to bring an end to a world. To me at that age they did.

As a child, conflict, to me, had meant misery and destroyed innocence, and sadly it still meant the same. Haunted still some thirteen years on, no I didn't like conflict and I didn't want to encounter it again. Senseless and upsetting, conflict, I decided, was something to be avoided if life was to be happy and peaceful. I could remember thinking these same thoughts that night on the landing. Aware today that I'd been unaware of losing my mind in order to avoid conflict, I had no idea how often I'd avoided it in my past. Quite often I suspected but I didn't really know. Definitely I feared conflict as much as I always had anger and probably by pretending that conflict too didn't exist, again I'd created a false security for myself. Allowing me to live the fragile life I had, without encountering conflict I'd never learnt to understand its role within effective communication. I'd never picked up any skills to deal with conflict and I'd never considered what conflict avoidance might be doing to me.

In the short term, by providing me with a means for getting out of awkward or unpleasant situations, avoiding conflict had always served me quite well. In the longer term however, with hindsight into the problems that avoiding anger had provided me, I could see that it hadn't actually done me any favours. The only thing that I'd managed to secure for myself, by refusing to confront conflict, was continued fear. I'd denied myself the right to healthy self-assertion and by choosing to leave many issues unresolved, I'd created confusion, uncertainty and a great deal of unnecessary anguish. As another consequence of having avoided conflict, I now also found myself in the vulnerable and rather primitive position of not knowing how to handle it effectively at all.

Unsure of how best to address this particular problem, and in sensing that this issue was going to be a big one, I decided to put the issue of conflict avoidance on hold until after I'd dealt with the laxatives. I managed to convince myself that by doing so I was responsibly managing my needs by prioritising issues as deemed appropriate. If the truth be known, in fact I was copping out.

November 2nd, 1990

Feedback time. Today when we re-assembled as usual on a Friday to report upon progress made during the week, I had very little to say. Knowing full well that I'd stated on Monday that I was going to spend this week looking for strategies to overcome my laxative abuse, I knew even better that I hadn't. Frantically trying to think up a valid excuse to justify what had after all been deliberate avoidance, I blamed the conflict issue for something or other and promised to carry my intention forward until the next week. Wimp.

If the rest of the group seemed satisfied that my reasoning was honourable, I myself remained unconvinced. My days at St. Andrew's were now numbered, I was still addicted to laxatives and I still greatly feared conflict. I had a lot of learning to put into practice and a lot of serious thinking to do.

Tonight I drove up to Dundee to spend the weekend with Roger. I hadn't seen him for over a month and I was dying to see him. I'd missed him more than ever. Deprived of the closeness that I shared only with him, I'd missed too his love and caring and I was longing to feel special again. So much had happened since we'd last been together and I could hardly wait to see his face when he saw how much better I was. Longing just to grab hold of him and to see his smile and hear his voice properly, I'd looked forward to tonight for as many days and nights as we'd been apart. Dreaming myself ahead of the journey and knowing exactly what to expect on my arrival, I couldn't wait to be scooped up and buried safely in Roger's arms. I couldn't wait to be spoiled either and to have him and his undivided attention, all to myself for two whole days. Perfect.

Wanting to be there *now*, I left York buzzing. Deliberately leaving my laxatives behind me, this weekend I decided was going to be a good one and I was going to enjoy myself. Even if it killed me. Drowning myself relentlessly in New Order for the first hour and a half of the drive, by the time I reached Newcastle I decided to opt for silence instead for a while. Bringing with it time to think, this maybe wasn't the wisest of moves. My weekend with Roger had been planned for ages and my journey well thought out in advance. My decision to leave my supply of laxatives in York, had not, and by Edinburgh I was having severe withdrawal pangs. Leaving the city lights behind me and with them a last chance of obtaining a fix for the night, I honestly wondered what the hell I was doing. Driving into the unknown is probably an apt description.

Bleak at the best of times, pitch black and no doubt barren too, the monotony of the road before me did nothing to distract or brighten my thoughts. Ambling through the miles and miles of blackened hills that rambled on and on before me, without realising what I was doing I found myself muttering about dark satanic hills. 'Jerusalem', having survived my abhorration of forced assemblies at school, was the only hymn that I'd ever held any kind of liking for. That I should find myself incorrectly reciting it whilst lost in the middle of Blackadder River land, did not reassure me that I was of rational mind. Irrationality of course was well within my forte and indeed had been for a long time. Singing hymns was not, and quite frankly this behaviour perturbed me. Hymns for God's sake – me? Bloody hell. If irrationality was a weird thing, then laxative deprivation promised an interesting weekend if nothing else.

It was almost midnight when I finally arrived in Dundee. Driving across the Tay Bridge leaving the darkness behind me, I allowed the lights of the Dundee sky-line to steal my thoughts. Reminding myself that I'd not driven 250 miles to be miserable, for Roger's sake if not my own, I made a pact with myself to divert my thoughts away from laxatives and feeling fat, at least until I was back in York.

As I turned the corner into Abbotsford Place I saw Roger's shadow disappear from the window. Suddenly feeling very much awake, I jumped out of the car and was immediately swept off my feet by the huge black jumper, that had somehow negotiated four flights of stairs in about ten seconds to greet me. Lost in the warmth and security of the strength that towered above me, I felt safe and I felt wanted. Lovingly protected from the big bad world that normally surrounded me, I'd found my escape and I was going to get the best from it. Bounding me back up the stairs as daft as a puppy in a strange house, I didn't need to ask if Roger was as happy to see me as I was him. Hugging and hugging me, swinging me round and then hugging me again, his actions said it all. Knocking a mug of tea off the table as he waltzed me from his room to the kitchen, the things I loved most about him hadn't changed. Still as mad and as haphazard as ever, he was just the same. Clumsy and big footed, fun, funny and always smiling, he was the perfect antidote for my miserable thoughts, and all that I wanted.

Talking and talking until well after four in the morning, tonight I got real pleasure from telling Roger all about the progress that I felt I'd made. Sharing what I'd learned about myself and my 'ineffectivenesses', as I described how I was beginning to work upon becoming more assertive, I don't think Roger could quite believe what he was hearing. Clearly over the moon at having evidence (after all this time) to suggest that I *was* beginning to beat my anorexia, he told me that he felt confident for the first time that I would recover. Thrilled to bits, he said he could see it happening and told me that he was prouder of me than I'd ever know.

Completely contented, having talked the two of us to sleep, when I awoke the next morning I felt even better. Waking up knowing that someone else was proud of something that I'd done had given me the greatest feeling of achievement, and I felt really secure and good about myself. I also felt better for having slept all night without having to entertain the laxatives. Lying awake with Roger snoring blissfully beside me was proof enough to me that I could survive one night without the things, but could I survive two? When I did and awoke on Sunday morning without any of the side effects that I'd expected, I couldn't quite believe that nothing had happened. I'd deliberately not eaten much the day before, but even so I was amazed to find my stomach flat enough to satisfy even my standards. Feeling that for once luck had been on my side, I could only conclude that for some reason the documented effects of laxative withdrawal had managed to escape me.

Amazed not only by this but also by how much I'd enjoyed the entire weekend, marking a definite milestone, the last few days had been the best that Roger and I had spent together. Whereas up until now, my anorexia had dictated and dominated the nature and scheduling of everything that we'd done during the four years we'd been together, this weekend it hadn't. We hadn't been restricted by the self-doubts and paranoia that normally told me to avoid situations where people might see and dislike me. I hadn't spent hours each morning despairing at trying to decide what to wear, so as not to look fat or odd or conspicuous. I'd been able to relax and I hadn't felt inferior to any of Roger's friends. For two days we'd managed to plan everything around morning, afternoon and evening, rather than breakfast, lunch and tea. We'd eaten in, Roger had eaten out whilst I'd had coffee and I'd coped with the nightmare of eating at strange times, in strange places and with strange cutlery. We'd been able to spend the whole of Saturday out and away from Roger's flat (or more specifically the loo) without me freaking, and we'd enjoyed a lovely day together driving through the mountains. We'd even managed on our return to join Roger's flat mates for a meal they'd cooked and although I ate very little, we'd both enjoyed that too.

Far more relaxed and less panicky than usual, where in the past I'd often been too tense and wound up to *really* enjoy being with Roger, this time the whole weekend had been lovely. Happier than I'd known us be together, there'd been no traumas, I hadn't felt out of control with anything and my anorexia had hardly been an issue. Thinking back a few months to the evening of Roger's May Ball when I'd panicked (because I'd felt too fat to wear a ball dress) and Roger had had to hang on to me to stop me jumping from his fourth floor window, by comparison, this weekend a lot had changed. Not wanting to leave but knowing that I had to, when Sunday arrived I left Roger and Dundee feeling sad that we were apart again but confidently happy that from now on everything was just going to get better and better.

Driving away from Dundee, I felt optimistic that defeating laxatives would be a piece of cake. I should have known better. Convinced that the lower section of my seat belt was buried further within the folds of skin that constituted my stomach than usual, again as I reached Edinburgh I felt decidedly uncomfortable. I also felt physically bloated and by the time I finally arrived back in York, I felt huge. It took me ten minutes to unload the car and unpack my bags. It took me all night to stop crying. Everything seemed so unfair, so cruel. Why? Why me? Two days without the dreaded dose of misery. Two nights of uncertainty and fears unfounded. An afternoon of elation and now this.

Forcing what seemed like hundreds of disgusting yellow pills down my throat, I longed for the release that I only hoped they'd bring. I'd eaten only two apples all day, I knew that there was nothing in my system for the laxatives to work upon and I realised that swallowing the bloody things was futile. I knew that the night ahead would be sheer hell and that I wouldn't sleep. I knew it all but I was beyond myself. I was desperate.

November 5th, 1990

Feeling that I'd never be able to live without laxatives, this morning I returned to St. Andrew's believing that there was little point in me carrying on anymore. Out of a sense of duty and nothing else, when it came to my turn to voice my intention for the week ahead, I muttered something about trying to convince myself that giving up laxatives would be worthwhile. My words were a blatant lie.

Betrayed and disillusioned, I had no intention of trying to persuade myself that dropping laxatives would be worth anything. Last night had given me all the evidence I needed to know that life without laxatives could never be worth living. Stupid enough to trick myself into going against my better judgement once, no way was I going to try kidding myself again. I'd lost my enthusiasm to fight and I felt totally disgusted and worthless. Bloated and fat, today I couldn't even be bothered to share how I was feeling with the group. I didn't want to face the fact that I was looking towards defeat. In cruel reality, reaching that point would mean that once again I'd failed and I couldn't take failure anymore.

Feeling desperately in need of some decent self-pity, I wanted to be alone. I was well pissed off with life.

November 6th, 1990

Today the drama session turned into a psychodrama exercise whereby I tried to experiment with giving up laxatives, using the support of the group to explore different options and risks.

Dividing the room up into three areas, **A**, **B** and **C**, (as shown in the Drama Session Room Plan below) I was encouraged to visualise each as a stopping stage in the journey of my life.

– **A** represented where I was presently (at St. Andrew's, safe but stuck)
– **B** revisited my past and represented the depressed state that I'd experienced when I'd constantly felt both hungry and fat
– **C** represented some place in my future, a happy place controlled by me and not the laxatives

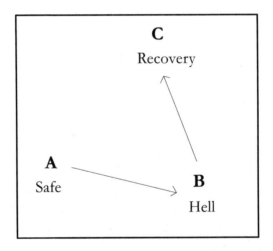

Drama Session Room Plan

Beginning at **A**, I was asked to experiment moving from my 'stuckness' towards the place where I wanted to be, **C**, verbalising my thoughts as I moved across the room. Since I could only travel to **C** from **B**, the experiment deliberately involved me leaving my safe place behind me in order to revisit the hell of my past, on route to **C**. Moving from **A** to **B** was a journey that I already knew. I'd encountered it briefly at the weekend and had not enjoyed the experience. I found the progression from relative sanity to feeling fat and out of control, even in the context of the experiment, unpleasant. I was physically reluctant to walk towards the part of the room representing the hell of my past, but was encouraged to continue walking until I actually arrived at **B.** Taking my thoughts immediately back to the depressed nightmarish life that I'd endured before finding laxatives, exercise only or not, I hated being there. Faced with moving towards the future (since I associated being happy and recovered with being fat and other entities unknown) in reality I did not want to risk moving towards **C.** I wanted to be happy and thin and from where I was standing, although using laxatives was unacceptable, **A** certainly seemed the less scary option.

Standing in the middle of a room, surrounded by furniture representing life zones and people who were probably wondering what the hell I was doing, I found myself wondering the same. I didn't voice my thoughts but I thought the exercise was stupid. I couldn't see any point in it and I wasn't exactly sure as to why I was going along with it. When asked to move from **B** to **C**, a journey that I'd never encountered before, keen to keep the drama therapist happy, I pretended to describe feelings that I thought would signify to her that the experiment was not the dead loss that I was allowing it to be. Still convinced that the experiment was useless, to my amazement as I reached a point about five steps away from the window that represented place **C**, I found myself unable to move any further. To me this was even more ridiculous than the experiment itself. I couldn't explain why my feet wouldn't move nor why my mind should simultaneously freeze, but they wouldn't and it did.

Lost within the conspiracy of my crazed mind, the experiment ceased to be. Rooted to the spot, my make believe future scared me too much to be stupid anymore. I couldn't understand what was happening, I felt extremely uneasy and I was powerless to do anything. The group, dispersed all around me, volunteered their support and bombarded me with positive affirmations, but despite their strength I still felt as though I couldn't move. Given the opportunity to leave everything behind me, had I been in my right mind I would have jumped at the chance of walking into a life totally devoid of anorexia, laxatives and their associated misery. But strangely, almost as though part of me didn't want to let go, I found myself unprepared even to flirt with the future.

Haunted by the depressive memories of past despair and unconcerned that I was probably destroying my body, my decision to abuse laxatives had been a conscious one. They'd provided me with a mechanism to avoid 'fat' days and had paradoxically promoted a feeling of well-being which I knew before long could quite easily kill me. Breaking my addiction would bring about a new set of circumstances. It would also leave me completely exposed. Torn between retreating back to square one (a place I would not wish upon anybody), and stepping forward into the unknown, I could not convince myself that either option was acceptable. My apparent inability to override restrictive thought processes, once confined only within my subconscious, had now shifted to involve both my conscious and motor control. And this clearly posed a threat to future progress.

I'd come up against a huge mental block which as a means of self-protection, for once I could fully understand. In not wanting to stop using laxatives but knowing that at some stage I had to, by blocking constructive planning, my head was ruling my actions for me and taking the easy way out. As stubborn as I was, the game that my mind was playing I knew would be extremely difficult to defeat. Breaking my addiction with laxatives was going to be hell.

Far from gaining strength and determination from the experiment I'd just undertaken, the only thing that today's drama session did for me was reinforce my 'stuckness' and emphasise the sheer size of the problem laxatives posed for me. Tonight I felt disheartened beyond belief and totally floored. Doubting I had anything like the courage I imagined I'd need to face life without laxatives, my overall aim now seemed impossible. Unable to see beyond my block I just couldn't see how life without laxatives could ever be worthwhile. Failing, I honestly didn't know whether I'd ever beat my anorexia. Terrified that I wouldn't and that I'd be trapped forever, miserable and depressed, if I needed a reason to complete my writing, I needed it now.

Dreading what I was about to put myself through, tonight at around midnight I felt momentarily strong. Deciding there and then that I would finish this book, all I had to do, I convinced myself, was keep writing.

November 7th, 1990

In more ways than one, despite what seemed an ominous future, today was quite an enjoyable day. Having started off with what had become a weekly dose of watery chaos, I thoroughly enjoyed thrashing about in the pool for an hour. Quite simply, it made a pleasant change from thrashing about in my head and since swimming was always followed by a huge coffee break back at the hospital, as far as I was concerned it was certainly an OK way to start the day.

Sitting quietly in the coffee lounge this morning, much to my amusement, I learnt that along with everyone else I'd apparently scared a set of workmen to such a degree that they didn't dare come anywhere near me. Commissioned by the Health Authority to repair a couple of doors at St. Andrew's, the workmen in question, having already postponed their arrival on three prior occasions, had then phoned to demand nurse protection for themselves before finally refusing to come at all. Looking around the room with real affection, knowing everyone as well as I did I honestly don't think I'd ever before been part of a more harmless set of people. That anyone should be scared of us collectively, was laughable. That a set of burly workmen should be scared of me – a self-confessed seven-stone-pacifist-come-weakling – greatly entertained me and for the rest of the day pushed all other thoughts from my mind.

November 8th, 1990

Motivated once more into looking for the brighter side of life, today in the small group session I tried to look towards the future positively rather than negatively. I found this difficult, and Katie suggested that I might like to create an 'I want list', detailing within reachable limits every hope and dream that I'd ever wished for. Highlighting the importance of needing to know where I was heading, having used this particular strategy herself some years before hand, Katie described how, by learning to identify and slowly satisfy a list of achievable wants, she'd helped herself through a difficult time. By using the example of how she had moved from the South of England to live in a cottage in the Dales, Katie demonstrated that with effort and direction it was actually possible to fulfil even seemingly impossible aspirations. On a smaller scale, she also pointed out the benefits to be derived from setting and satisfying everyday 'wants' on a regular basis.

Having never really allowed myself the luxury of 'selfishly' thinking about what I wanted out of life, the notion of fulfilling personal dreams seemed alien to me. For a start, apart from wanting to get rid of my anorexia, I didn't have any personal dreams. I wanted to make everyone around me happy, I wanted to stop causing endless worry to my parents and Roger, and I wanted to be liked by everyone – but that was about all. Materialistically there wasn't anything that I wanted. I had clothes, a roof over my head and no genuine reason to starve. I had friends, music and plenty to do. Money wasn't important to me and I didn't need anything. The only thing I'd ever really wanted apart from love and security, was to study medicine but that was something I couldn't have anyway. I'd failed at that well and truly and since there was nothing else I wanted to do, I'd had no aspirations for anything achievement-wise either.

Sensing a kind of empty loss inside of me, slowly it began to dawn on me why it should be that I always felt that I wasn't getting anything out of life. Having often questioned what point there was to living other than to provide happiness for others, suddenly I could see why I'd come to view life as a disappointment. Instead of reaching out and grabbing for what ever I wanted, disillusioned into taking a back seat, I'd allowed any dreams that I might once have had to become redundant and lost. Without dreams, I'd lost all sense of meaningful reason and celebration, and I'd come to view life as a disappointment quite simply because I'd never allowed it to become anything but.

Glancing around the room, my eyes met with equally disillusioned others. Recognising in myself an eagerness to replenish the lost years of emptiness, I wanted desperately to get beyond the discontented dreamlessness that had clung to me for too long. Quite excited by the prospect of somehow determining a kinder future, built out of hope and self-fulfilling prophecy, I also felt saddened. Saddened at realising how easy it was to fall into the trap of never asking for desires and needs to be met, and saddened because I found myself wondering just how many people in this world live and die, never having found direction. Never having found their dreams.

Today I weighed seven stone and two pounds.

November 9th, 1990

This evening, when I called to collect a sick-note from my GP, I asked him to explain to me exactly what I might experience from giving up laxatives. Aware of my fears of gaining weight in fluids, he patiently explained that initially I would retain quite a lot of fluid but that once initial rehydration had taken place, I'd then lose the remaining excess fluid that my body no longer needed. He estimated that this fluid imbalance might take up to three weeks to right itself, during which time he admitted I might well experience both bloating and a substantial gain in weight. He assured me that the initial increase in weight would eventually subside and stressed to me that what I seemed to foresee in terms of weight gain, was probably hugely exaggerated. He reinforced to me that he could fully understand my fears and although the precarious position that I'd landed myself in might more readily have justified impatience, as usual I met with none.

If laxatives were killing me Dr Markham probably knew that better than anyone. And certainly better than me, he also knew how ineffective they were as an aid to weight loss. Whilst I'd become addicted to dangerously playing about with my internal fluid balance, my body had become increasingly efficient at grabbing nutrients regardless of the speed that they passed through my system. I knew that my laxative addiction was not actually achieving anything. I knew only too well the destruction and metabolic chaos that I was forcing myself to endure and yet still I was allowing all sensible knowledge to fall on deaf ears. Nothing that Dr Markham said was new to me and yet I simply couldn't accept that what he was saying could possibly be true for me.

I had enough understanding to logically work out that coming off laxatives need not be the traumatic experience that I imagined it to be. I could see that life beyond laxatives was possible. I had proof that it was possible – I'd spoken to others who had managed to stop using them. But that wasn't me. No doubt everybody else would normalise as expected and go on to lead a text book life, eating normal food in normal amounts, whilst managing to remain abnormally thin. But I could guarantee that none of this would happen for me. Me? I'd gain far more fluid than anybody else. I'd never normalise, nor lead the text book life enjoying with it its text book bloody diet. In order to survive my mind, the only mechanism that I'd have to fall back on would be to stop eating all together. Lindsay's law of irrational fat accumulation and distribution directly proportional to bizarre-thought thinking, would come into play once more and I'd end up back where I began. Fat. Fat and disgusting. Bloated, huge and horrible. Of course nobody else would experience my fate. Nobody else would swell out of all recognisable proportions, or suffer a mind as fat as mine. For certain, mine would be the only body and brain not to respond as expected. I could guarantee it. Whilst everything always ran smoothly for everyone else, things only ever ran cruelly for me. That was how I felt anyway.

Restricted by my own pessimism, it wasn't until Dr Markham pointed out that I wouldn't necessarily have to alter the amount that I was presently eating in order to retain a stable weight once I'd come off the laxatives, that I began really to listen to what he or anybody had been saying. If it was true as he was predicting, that laxatives were probably no more than 5 to 10 per cent efficient, theoretically that would mean that I could continue to safely eat 90 to 95 per cent of the 1,200 calories a day, that had become the norm for me. It couldn't possibly be true but if things could only be that simple it would be brilliant. All I'd have to do to ensure I didn't gain weight would be to drop my calories from 1,200 to 1,080 per day. I wouldn't have to worry about gaining weight and becoming fat. I'd have nothing to fear, I could continue eating more or less what I was already, I wouldn't have to starve, I'd be able to sleep at night, I wouldn't be dehydrated, I wouldn't risk death and I wouldn't get depressed. Hell it would be the answer to everything, but it couldn't be that simple could it?

Convinced that it couldn't, I didn't know what to believe anymore and I didn't know what to think. Dr. Markham was trying to kid me. Surely he was lying to trick me. Playing on my ignorance in order to make me do something I didn't want to do. Liar. He wasn't telling me the truth. How could he be? Or was he? Was he telling me the truth? Could it be true? Could things really work out as he'd said? Bollocks. He was lying. He must be. If coming off laxatives was as easy as he was predicting, he'd have told me ages ago. No, he was trying to get me to trick myself. He must be. Would he do that? He wouldn't would he? Would he?

Recognising my reluctance to consider the judgement of others above my own, tonight I decided to force myself to believe that laxatives were as ineffective as Dr. Markham had said. He had after all only ever been honest with me in the past and he knew how scared I was. I also knew that I could trust him. He wasn't the sort to deliberately try to mislead me. Anyway, he knew me well enough to know that his life probably wouldn't be worth living if he did.

November 11th, 1990

Excited by the prospect of eating responsibly again without half killing myself in the process, today I saw hope no longer running towards the horizon with its arse still burning. Determined that I would stop using laxatives, today I tried to convince myself that beating laxatives was a battle that I could win. Looking for inspiration and proof that achieving the impossible did not always have to be just that, I thought back to one particular sunny day in July 1985:

Please remember this day all your lives. It's important.
Remember the day you wanted to help.
Remember the bands and crews who did it. The professionals
who made it all an extraordinary technological feat.
Remember the dying who were allowed to live.
Remember on the day you die, there is someone alive in
Africa 'cos one day you watched a pop concert.
Remember your tears and your joy.
Remember the love.
Remember on that day for once in our bloody lives WE WON.

Remember that even though it's over, it need not stop.
Remember the dying goes on and remember so that as time
passes you can tell others 'it's possible, I know'.
What a day, what a lovely day.

Bob Geldof, *Live Aid*, July 13th, 1985

I remembered that day for a number of reasons; certainly it had not
passed without leaving its mark upon me. Poignantly moved by an
overwhelming sense of shame that, whilst others had no choice, I
was actually choosing not to feed myself properly, I cried many tears.
Selfish and useless tears that achieved nothing. And whilst I cried,
so did the world. Bloody hell, if one man could orchestrate a global
event raising hundreds of millions of pounds to feed the starving;
if one man could unite the world with heart felt compassion and
bring everyone together even if just for one day; if he could do all
that, then the very least I could do was to stop feeling sorry for
myself and to learn once more how to feed myself without using
laxatives. Determined that for once in my life I was going to bloody
win and, inspired into kicking myself into action, using faith in human
nature as all the inspiration I needed, I decided to make my impossible
happen. It was about time I sorted myself out.

Shamed into finally doing something to help myself, my fears
could no longer be justified. The two-year bout of chronic diarrhoea
that I'd voluntarily prescribed myself, had been a complete waste
of time, energy and hurting. It had achieved nothing, my body had
learnt to compensate for all that I was doing and now I'd had enough.
Things were going to change.

Feeling angry that nobody had ever forced me to this point of
thinking before and cheated that my body had again tricked my
mind, I looked forward to the day that I could honestly say laxatives
were behind me.

November 12th, 1990
Despite now seeing laxatives in a slightly different light to that which
I had before, realistically there was still one thing holding me back
from dropping laxatives for good. My ever-morbid fear of gaining

weight. Realising that now would be as good a time as any to begin questioning what exactly it was about gaining weight that frightened me, this morning I told the group that I intended to look at my body image in relation to both my self-esteem and the fears which constantly seemed to surround me.

For years I'd lived the yo-yo existence whereby I felt confident and happy or miserable and a wreck, depending upon whether I perceived myself to be thin or fat. Stamped upon and trodden into the size-related image that I had of myself, my self-esteem hadn't stood a chance. Flourishing only when my body withered and waned, I needed to understand why my self-esteem always diminished when I tended back towards normality. Dreading the answers that I was no doubt about to find out, I deliberately didn't give today's intention much thought. Not knowing what the hell was going to happen when I stopped using the laxatives, I didn't want to spend time contemplating anything before I had to.

November 14th, 1990

Determined to stop using laxatives before the coming weekend, I used today's small group session to voice my fears about gaining the initial weight as fluid, which I knew would be unavoidable. I also asked the group for suggestions and possible strategies that I might adopt, to help me cope with what I knew would be a hellish couple of weeks.

Having abused and more importantly stopped abusing laxatives herself, one member of the group talked me through what she'd experienced on giving them up. Describing feelings that I could well imagine, she explained that she'd coped with the initial fluid retention purely by putting it down to something that was temporarily physically wrong with her. Rather than looking at the fluid gain in terms of weight gain, she described how instead she'd actually managed to talk her mind into blaming her weight increase upon a swollen liver. This in turn she'd convinced herself she could do nothing about. Attracted to the notion of developing or falling victim to an enlarged liver (a condition worthy of concern and not self-blame, were it to inflict anyone else), selfishly the thought of having something to feel genuinely sorry for myself for, appealed to me. I didn't know whether my mind would let it work, but as a short term coping strategy it was the best suggestion that I or anyone else could come up with.

Obviously stuck for further ideas or strategies, after a while when the group had fallen silent, Katie suggested that I might find it useful to analyse my behaviour, in terms of personal strengths which I might rely upon and weaknesses that I might change, in order to help me cope more efficiently. Partly due to me still believing that socially it was more acceptable to underplay personal qualities than to admit to and broadcast them, today in being quick to identify a substantial number of personal weaknesses but slow to acknowledge any strengths, I realised that my self-esteem was not what it should have been. Picking up on a couple of weaknesses that I'd not identified, and perhaps knowing me a little better than I did myself, Katie encouraged me to look at the difficulties I had with asking for help and acknowledging that people cared about me. Although I'd never considered either of these points before, when I thought about it, I realised that I'd had problems with both issues for as long as I could remember.

With respect to the former, asking for help was something that I very seldom found myself able to do. Suggesting weakness or failure on my part, admitting to myself that I couldn't cope alone was bad enough. Admitting to others that I needed help was even worse and not a skill that came to me naturally. Worried that I'd scare people off if I burdened them with problems which I felt I should have been able to sort out myself, there were very few people that I'd ever felt able to ask help from. I knew that Roger was always there for me and whenever I cried or got upset, he was always the person that I turned to first. Offering me love and constant support, he was always more than happy to help me with whatever, but as willing as he was, I never felt that I deserved his care and I always felt guilty after receiving it. Besides Roger, there were probably dozens of people who I could have turned to for help but only two that I ever did. Probably because I felt they knew me better than anyone except Roger, occasionally I'd turned to Caryn and Chris for help, but only when I'd been really upset.

But why did I need to cry to ask for help and why, as I was just beginning to realise, did I need to be upset to acknowledge that people cared about me? When it came to feeling loved and cared for, I could see that I'd always been very much loved and very much cared for. The problem was that I often didn't feel it. Creating a discrepancy which wasn't fair on those trying to love me, as if I'd been trying to deny myself those feelings of security that everything about my life should have provided me, I seldom ever allowed myself the luxury of feeling either loved or cared for. Disturbed into believing that I was worthy of neither, I only allowed myself to feel loved or cared for when I felt and could justify that I deserved it. And because I'd taken to not valuing anything that I ever did, I seldom felt that I deserved care and attention and I seldom dared to allow myself to accept either. When I did and usually when I was upset, I would convince myself that rather than being loved and cared for, for just being me, instead I was being loved out of some kind of duty or pity or bonded obligation.

I'd taken to believing that those close to me loved me purely because they had little choice in the matter. Preferring not to kid myself that anybody might love me out of choice, this kind of thinking felt safe. Love whose validity could be explained was, I decided therefore, a fairly safe risk. It couldn't go away. Love that depended upon me doing something to deserve it however, was a different story. It was, I decided, not guaranteed. It could be removed from or denied me and I couldn't cope with that risk. And so despite having no valid reason to justify my thinking, my parents, who clearly loved me and always had done, only did so because they were my parents. I was their daughter and so they had to love me. Even Roger I felt only loved me because he was under some obligation to do so. Initially yes, he might have loved me out of choice, but then I became 'Clare his girlfriend' and in my stupid head, having assumed a new identity, everything had changed.

Furthermore, and with respect to friends, I also realised that I only ever allowed myself to feel valued or cared for by them on those occasions when one or other of them behaved in such a way as to *prove* to me that they did care about me. But whether I was upset or not my friends did care. And although my self-esteem did its best to convince me otherwise, deep down my many memories couldn't deceive me. Thinking back, I remembered the freezing winter's day when Ravi had taken his jumper off and given it to me because he'd noticed me shivering. I remembered too the look of concern on his face the day I'd called into the pharmacy, where unbeknown to me he was working at the time, to pick up anti-depressants. I remembered Scott jumping over a wall, chasing after and catching a school kid and then washing his face in the snow, because the rather large brat had hit me with a snowball. I thought of the day that Nick had hugged me when I'd said I felt fat and I remembered Chris and Andrew trying to convince me that I wasn't. I remembered Chris sitting for ages trying everything possible to make me see myself how he claimed everyone else did; and I remembered the times when he'd picked me up, probably to check my weight without me knowing. I remembered Caryn dragging me off to the South of France in order to get me away from everything. I remembered her striving always to build my confidence and to make me laugh; and I remembered too her telling me that she knew of no one who everyone cared for more than they did me. I remembered Chris grabbing and pulling me back towards himself, Roger and Caryn at a concert, when I'd lost my footing to the crowd and had become separated from where they were standing. I remembered Scott carrying me across the bottom of a slimy waterfall to stop me from slipping; and I remembered Roger and Chris retrieving me from a tree in which I'd got stuck. I remembered Nick and Ravi reminding me that no matter what happened, they and the others would always be there for me; and then there were my memories of The Kirk and, of course, Roger.

Everything Roger did, when I took the care to think about it, made me feel special. With every breath he took he loved me and it was obvious. Even when I didn't feel deserving of his care and attention and couldn't admit to myself that it existed, it was always there. Realising consciously that the care of my friends continued too, regardless of what I did in return or whether I felt I deserved it or not, I began to see just how self-defeating my whole attitude to life had become. Thinking it too much of a coincidence that I should find myself stuck within a deeply unhappy pattern of behaviour, whilst I associated deserving to be cared for and loved with being upset and in need of attention, it slowly began to dawn on me that I might actually be getting a kick out of being miserable. But that was warped. In fact it was so warped that it couldn't possibly be true. And anyway, even if it was, what exactly did this realisation have to do with me giving up laxatives?

I didn't want it to be true.

November 15th, 1990

Perhaps sensing that I was as close as I'd ever be towards making the one realisation that I really needed, to both understand my anorexia and to let it go, this afternoon Katie chose 'the benefits of stress' as the focus for discussion in the awareness session. Working individually, we were each asked to look at what we might be gaining from being stressed. Having always seen myself as anorexic rather than stressed, I decided that it would be easier and more useful for me to look at what I gained from being anorexic.

So what was I gaining from being anorexic? This seemed a stupid question to me. I wasn't getting anything from being anorexic. I hated everything to do with my eating disorder. The starving, the craving, vomiting, the laxatives, exercise, the sleepless nights, hunger, self-loathing, the waking up and wishing I hadn't – I despised it all. A forced lifestyle, a restricted me. I hated it with a passion. I didn't get anything from being anorexic. What could I, or anybody for that matter, possibly get out of feeling fat, depressed, guilty, ineffective, feeble, useless, pathetic, hungry, confused and pissed off – constantly? Yeah, I was gaining a load from being anorexic. It was doing wonders for me. Fat chance. If I was getting anything from my eating disorder, why was I always so bloody miserable? And then it clicked. 'Miserable'. If it was possible to get a kick out of being miserable, maybe I was getting a kick out of being anorexic as well.

Without doubt I had used my anorexia as a coping mechanism: a strategy for avoiding painful issues, an excuse for hiding rather than confronting and a means for maintaining control. Realising that I'd used it too as a reason to feel sorry for myself and maybe even to secure love and care, it suddenly dawned on me that I'd allowed my illness to become a sole means of attracting attention. Horrified by this admission, I felt dreadful. Selfish. Spoilt. Brat. Horrible child. Attention seeker. Show-off. Totally ashamed, the childhood messages and images that I'd done everything to avoid as a child, flooded back and I felt unable to escape. Momentarily trapped within the same mind that had dictated good and bad to me as a seven-year-old, I felt as though I'd committed every bad deed known to man and had just been caught.

The truth hurt and I didn't like it.

Strangely enough though, I'd never particularly wanted to seek attention. In fact the contrary, for years I'd been deliberately covering up much of my behaviour for fear of being seen to attract more than my fair share of attention. All I ever wanted out of life, was the security of knowing that I was important to other people and that those who mattered had reason to care for me. I needed to feel that I was well liked, that I was valued and that I was surrounded by people whose concern and protection I could depend upon. Now in realising and having to accept that much of my behaviour had been driven totally by selfish motives, I felt sick.

But being anorexic was safe. As a central focus in my life, for years my anorexia had provided an obstacle behind which I'd learned to shirk responsibilities; to shut off from everything around me; and to forget about those needs that I had which, subconsciously perhaps, I feared not being met. Additionally, whilst my pursuit of thinness controlled my self-esteem and so often caused me despair, occasionally it rewarded me by means of achievement and maybe self-satisfaction. Always too, by seeing my situation as unique to me and maybe intriguing to others, my anorexia set me apart from everybody else and even made me feel special. And I needed that. I needed attention too and to feel that I was loved and cared for. I didn't, however, want or need to be the centre of attention anywhere, it wasn't that so much that my behaviour craved, but rather constant reassurance.

Whether this particular belief was fact or not, it didn't really matter. At the end of the day, the important thing was that finally

I'd come to understand why my anorexia had become such a central part of my life.

I hated to think of myself as an attention seeker. Everyone hated attention seekers. Weighing seven stone and one pound, this evening I decided would be the last that I'd use laxatives.

November 16th, 1990

Sharing my unease at realising quite how selfish I'd become in using my anorexia to harness attention, today I found out that I hadn't been the only one left feeling guilty.

Feeling slightly better for knowing that my thoughts hadn't been very different to anyone else's, today I was knocked back again by something another client said. Contrasting my belief that being ill brought me attention, she described how in her experience it had noticeably driven attention from her. Something I'd never considered before, her comment forced me to think again about the effect that my anorexia was having on everyone around me. But my being ill I was sure had never frightened my friends away. Or had it? Maybe my being anorexic had made me difficult to talk to and scary to know. And maybe I was too falsely happy or too serious or too wrapped up in myself for others to feel comfortable with me. Not wanting to think that any of this might be true, I remembered Chris once telling me that although he and everybody else had noticed and had been concerned about my weight loss, no one had dared approach me about it.

Sending my mind spinning, I began wondering whether my anorexia had distanced me from everyone. If it had, in terms of satisfying my needs, this would mean that my behaviour was actually far less effective than I presently perceived it to be. Shocked into realising that this was quite possible, I felt cheated, pretty confused and almost angry. Strangely however, rather than this being a setback, probably because I was fed up with playing games which seemed unfair, if anything, the uncertainty of it all angered me enough to view giving up laxatives as some kind of rebellion. So with blissful ignorance, I did it. I gave them up.

November 17th, 1990

As if giving up the use of laxatives was not traumatic enough, tonight just as the first effects were beginning to affect me, Roger and I (both home for the weekend) returned to The Kirk. I shouldn't have gone.

Substantially renovated, everything about the place that had once endeared me had now been ripped away. The blackened walls and the darkened mysterious atmosphere that had always welcomed me, were now no more. No doubt tossed aside to make way for bigger and brighter things, the bending narrow stairways and twisted passageways which had once led reassuringly to the addictive trance of a pauper's dance floor, had gone too. Lost: the sympathetic lighting and subtle shadowed images that had once adorned my body and quietened my mind. No longer the haunt that had become a favourite place and launched a thousand memories. No longer a place where I could lose myself. Where once charismatic energy had echoed from the walls creating mystique amidst the darkness, now the only thing to bounce from the walls was me. Swallowed up by the damn things and spat back out by a nuisance of mirrors, my once dulled image, now amplified and fluorescing, refused not to torment me and wouldn't let me go.

Filled with unhappy faces trapped within lifestyles dictated by suits, this place which had once represented everything that my friends meant to me, had fallen. Lost to a sad upmarket monotony, destroyed. Ripping from me a past never to be lived again, I hated what the builders had done. A three million pound betrayal and nothing to show for it but floodlit chrome, spinning lights and uncomfortable people with the best times gone. Saddened beyond reason, the memories of evenings spent there that had once kept me going, could never be more than just that. Images irreplaceable, which I wanted more than anything to be part of me again. But no, I'd lost a friend. The part of me that had once felt safe had gone and I didn't feel safe anymore.

Driving home tonight I felt fat and secretly I cried.

November 18th, 1990

Catching a glimpse of myself in my bedroom mirror this morning confirmed my worst fears. I was huge. Climbing back into bed, mind agog with self-destructive thoughts, I realised that it had been quite a long time since I'd last felt as bad as I did. Irrationality drowned within a sea of fatty tissue which seemed content to swim freely beneath my skin. Lost too, my waist and hip bones, replaced unkindly by some cruel distended watery structure within which my self-esteem sank. Swollen legs and yoghurty arms; the rest of me unbearable; my chest repulsive. God what a mess. What a blubbery mess.

Punching and pummelling and squashing every bit of me that now squelched, I didn't know what to do. Totally disgusted with what had happened so quickly, today I felt too ashamed to face the world. Not daring to think about tomorrow, I spent much of the day in bed. Well away from observing eyes and well away from food.

November 19th, 1990
Beached Whale Status

Bastard world, I hate this. Why me, why can't I be thin? Everybody wants me to be fat, no one cares! What's the point? I can't win. I want to be thin – it's been taken from me – I want to die. Fuck this struggle, I've had enough. Hell I feel huge. Everything I've worked for, now I've lost. I might as well weigh twenty stone. I'll stuff my face, see if I care. I'm never going to lose this sodding water. Fluid retention, swollen liver or fat. How am I supposed to know what's going on? My body can't be trusted to work properly and my mind to believe what people say. I WANT TO SMASH MY ARM AGAINST THE WALL. I want to lose control. I'm going mad. All I can see is thin people all around me – why, why can't I be thin? Nobody understands. This is hell, what's the point? How can I be proud of anything I've achieved, how can I like myself, when all I feel is this?

November 20th, 1990

This morning I awoke to find four red roses sent from Dundee, to mark the fourth anniversary that Roger and I had been together.

Feeling even more bloated and swollen than the day before, I didn't feel that I deserved them. Saddened that I should feel so negative on what should have been a happy day, when I attempted to describe what I was experiencing to the members of my small group I became both confused and upset. What was happening to me? Everything had fallen apart and I didn't understand anything anymore. Roger's flowers were lovely; the thought behind them even more so, and I was the luckiest girl alive to have him and to know that he cared about me as much as he did, but today I didn't feel lucky. I just felt guilty and I didn't deserve flowers. I didn't deserve anything.

Feeling sorry for myself, today of all days I should have been celebrating but I couldn't be bothered. Too blocked out to even care that I was being completely selfish, I'd lost it. I felt fatter than even I could imagine and I didn't know whether I could stand it much more. I couldn't think straight, I couldn't sleep, I didn't dare eat and I felt as though every sodding cell in my body had imploded. I felt completely out of control – I was ballooning and ballooning and running out of skin. And all the time inside I was drowning. I didn't know where I was, who I was or what time of day it was, and I didn't want to either. The life had gone from me and I just didn't care.

Way out of touch with any sense of feeling, in the space of four days I'd fallen completely back into my old patterns of thinking and it scared me to think of how easy it had been. Realising that I needed to get behind the 'feeling fat' thoughts to really understand what was going on, I tried to work out what my mind was trying to block out, but couldn't. Terrified that I'd never feel OK again, I felt a little better for knowing that everyone at St. Andrew's was behind me. That they all felt willing to pick me up and support me, helped whilst I was at the hospital but not when I wasn't there.

Feeling desperate and suicidal, I dreaded being alone.

November 21st, 1990

I don't know where my thoughts were today but somehow I managed to drive myself to college instead of the hospital. Given that I'd not attended lectures for over four months and that I'd been driving to St. Andrew's almost daily for the last nine weeks, I thought this a strange thing to do. Concerned that I should drive anywhere without apparent awareness of what I was doing, nor with any recognition of anything that had gone through my mind on route, I half wondered whether I was still asleep. My eyes were open, I could see all around me and I knew that I was sitting in the wrong car park, but, as if I was watching somebody else behind the wheel of my car, I couldn't work out what was going on in the driver's head. Far from reassured that this was normal behaviour, like an unknown entity passing from one world into another, as though my consciousness was dead, I felt as if part of my mind had dissociated itself from my body. Being used to owning bizarre thoughts, I could not recall ever before thinking bizarre non-thoughts and in many ways I felt as though I was dreaming. Either that or I was going mad.

Talking with Katie having finally arrived at a correct destination, this morning she acknowledged many of the difficulties that I was experiencing and commented that I appeared to be coping very well under the circumstances. Impressed with how courageous and determined she claimed I was being, she pointed out that what I was experiencing now was the worst bit and added that it would just be a question of time before things would start to get better. Katie really seemed to appreciate what I was going through, and having decided not to weigh me (probably for fear of sending me to an early grave), told me that she was extremely proud of me for staying with my feelings and not giving up.

It had been a long time since anyone had said they were 'proud' of me and that word meant a lot. I needed to hear it. I needed to know that someone could see what I was going through and could recognise how hard the struggle had become. Instantly making me feel that my efforts weren't going unnoticed, I admired Katie for knowing exactly what to say. Her timing had been pretty good too and I gained definite strength from feeling that someone believed in me.

November 22nd, 1990

For a day that started out just like any other, today I had reason to celebrate. Marking the beginning of what I hoped to be a better era all round, for almost the first time since I'd stopped using laxatives, today I smiled. In fact to be perfectly honest, due to events catching me completely by surprise, I think it would be almost fair to say that I actually enjoyed myself today. I had two special people to thank. Firstly Nikki for throwing a surprise party to mark the eve of my twenty-second birthday and secondly, a significant other, whose one kind gesture perhaps touched the heart of the nation and certainly did mine.

Consequently, whilst I celebrated in York with friends, on the day that Mrs Thatcher finally stepped down, Roger got horribly drunk in Dundee, Dad took the day off work and Gary danced the night away at a 'Yes She's Gone' party in Bradford.

November 23rd, 1990

Reflecting upon the high spirits that had, in my opinion, quite rightly warmed much of the country the day before, in stark contrast and with energy flagging, my birthday seemed rather insignificant and passed with little excitement. Having struggled since Monday to eat 1,080 calories each day, convinced that I'd gained an enormous amount of weight, instead of being happy and worry free, I felt pretty depressed all day.

To make things worse I'd received some chocolates through the post and, feeling too fat to eat any of them, I couldn't stop thinking about them. Torn between putting one in my mouth and enjoying it, or mentally misdirecting the anger that really I had for myself towards the sender and life in general, I chose the lowest calorie option of the two and felt desperately sad that my thinking had become as low and as twisted as it had. I felt guilty too that so many people should go to the trouble of sending me cards and presents, when I had the audacity to not go out of my way to enjoy myself. I didn't deserve kindness today. I felt too miserable and grumpy. I felt ungrateful as well, but then, when everyone else always put more stock into my birthday than I ever did, feeling ungrateful had become inevitable.

Feeling badly that I'd let everyone down again, I hated birthdays, but most of all I hated myself for not being happy.

November 24th, 1990

Not wanting to know my weight but at the same time feeling that I could no longer cope with not having a definite value to judge my size by, today I weighed myself. Another reason for doing so, I convinced myself, was to deliberately catch my weight at its highest reading, so that when I finally lost the excess fluid, if I was left with a little weight gain it would seem insignificant by comparison and perhaps even bearable. It seemed a good idea in theory until I stood on the scales.

I couldn't believe it. I knew I'd put on weight but I'd no idea how much. A week ago I'd weighed seven stone and one pound, now the scales registered seven stone and thirteen pounds, and I couldn't cope. Seven-thirteen – God that was nearly eight stone. Twelve per cent. Hell, my weight had increased by 12 per cent. That meant that I was now nearly an eighth bigger than I had been. Shit.

Wanting to fling myself through the window, I settled instead for thrashing my arm against the corner of the door. Harder and harder. I needed something to dull the panic and to stop me thinking. I needed something to keep my thoughts from not wanting to live. Not knowing what to do, I threw everything into trying to break my arm. Bringing release until the damn thing turned numb, I'd tried. I'd tried so hard and yet I'd achieved nothing. I wasn't coping. I wasn't coping at all and I could see no point in carrying on. Frightened and betrayed, my thinner self had gone. Now I could only get fatter.

My arm ached like hell but tonight I was too screwed up even to feel sorry for myself.

November 25th, 1990

This morning I awoke remembering little of the day before. Besides standing on the scales and seeing the pointer way exceed the acceptable, I could recall nothing. The size of the bruise covering much of my upper arm gave some indication as to the depth of my feelings, but little else.

Perhaps cushioned for a while, my thoughts brought me no logical sense. Again I'd lost the ability to think spontaneously and again I was no longer aware of my feelings. From huge uncertainty, I'd regressed back to the familiarity and safeness that feeling fat had always trampled upon me. Blocking as much from my mind as was possible, I was hardly a conscious being. Like sleeping however, my numbed brain and dulled reactions gave me the release that I needed and I welcomed them. Dropping things and crying all the time without knowing why, today when I caught and burnt my arm in the steam trail from the kettle – and didn't feel it – I began to realise how unaware of everything I'd become. Scared that it could be possible to scald myself without knowing, tonight when I drove into town and returned home without my car (because I'd forgotten that I'd set out with it), I couldn't convince myself that I wasn't going mad.

Shamefully absorbed in me, me and me, today I didn't really think about Roger. Just two days after my own, today was his birthday and I'd forgotten. Brilliant girlfriend I was.

November 28th, 1990

As always one step ahead of me, having watched me make no progress since I'd given up laxatives, today Katie put to me an important ultimatum that really I needed to put to myself. Did I want to stay where I was now, unhappily controlled by weight but safe, or did I want to allow my body to normalise to its natural weight in order to find true happiness? Both options were unacceptable to me, and I felt trapped. But as usual when I thought about it, Katie was right. If my sanity was to remain intact I needed to decide what I really wanted. That said however, even the thought of her ultimatum disturbed me. I hated being unhappy but as I was I was simply too fat to consider accepting any further weight gain.

Feeling both threatened and angry, I wanted only for my bones to stick out again.

November 29th, 1990

Katie weighed me today prior to the small group session. Hoping against hope that my weight would be less than what it had been the weekend before, to my utter disgust it remained the same. Convinced that my body would never normalise, instantly I panicked and felt exactly as I'd done five days earlier when I'd first stood back on the scales. Overwhelmed again by suicidal thoughts which told me that death had to be better than life at that moment, once again I didn't know what to do. Katie tried to reassure me that it was still early days and that there was still time for the fluid and weight gain to subside, but I couldn't believe her. I felt fat and nothing anyone could say could take it away from me.

I took my panic with me into today's small group session, and this morning we spent the whole hour discussing me. Totally supported and surrounded by friends, everyone there knew what I was going through and in many ways they were living it with me. Today Katie pointed out to me that since I'd come off the laxatives I'd spoken only of food, feeling fat, and fears concerning my weight. I was stuck again and now more scared than I'd ever been. Adding that I'd not mentioned any of the issues that I'd previously worked upon, Katie suggested that maybe I'd feel less panicky if I stopped thinking only of issues centring around food. Deciding that this would in fact benefit everyone and not just me, when an 'anti-food' contract (aimed at discouraging food-talk during small group sessions) was proposed by one member of the group, the rest of us agreed it would be a good idea.

Realising that I had indeed been avoiding unresolved issues, tonight I sat for hours thinking really positively about trying to accept myself as I was, regardless of what I weighed. I tried to convince myself that weight didn't matter and that people wouldn't (as everybody said) view me differently if my weight changed, but I remained unsuccessful on both counts. To me weight did matter. And since I was secretly convinced that being thin brought me positive attention that automatically I would lose if I deviated too far from my former thinner self, I didn't want to believe the latter either.

I thought that, in the eyes of others, being anorexic gave me an identity that otherwise I would not have had. And since my illness and bizarre patterns of behaviour had become intricately entwined within my whole sense of being, I could not imagine myself as anything other than anorexic. What's more, in realising that I'd extended this line of thinking to involve those around me, I'd become convinced that everyone else viewed and judged me likewise as 'Clare the anorectic'. Extrapolating from this and oblivious to my ego-centricity, out of perversity more than anything else, my mind had arrived at the assumption that my weight and size were as important to everyone else as they were to me.

In fact for years, I had without permission been trespassing into the minds of others and distorting thoughts that weren't even mine. Twisting my perception in an attempt to place awareness and concern into the everyday thoughts of everybody else, effectively I'd created a mind of external thoughts from which I could steal feelings of worth whenever I wanted. Totally unaware of how self-centred my whole attitude had become, I'd created an illusion born of stubborn pretentiousness. A dangerous and unfunny game, whose extended rules had rapidly extended to rule me and within whose fat grasp I was still stuck. But however far from satisfactory this illusionary state of mind had become, it did at least partly explain why it should be that my weight had become a central focus in my quest for self-esteem. Living with the grossest of imaginations, I only ever held myself in high esteem when I felt thin enough to believe those messages of concern that I'd invented around me. Providing me with telling insight as to what had been going on inside my head, having clearly lost touch with reality, I realised that I had no idea how people really did view me and that scared me.

I needed to know exactly how everyone around me did perceive me and I needed to know whether my illness did, as I believed, play any part in shaping their perceptions. There were two possibilities. Either it did or it didn't. If it did, then everything I'd believed would be true and I'd have a lot to lose from giving up my anorexia. If, on the other hand, my anorexia did not alter how other people perceived me, the implications of this would be simply enormous. Not only would this mean that I was not as important to my friends as I had kidded myself into believing, it would also suggest that my being anorexic was not satisfying – at all – those needs I believed it was. Jumping straight into what I viewed to be the worst possible scenario, I felt incredibly sad and completely pissed off. Sad because my illusion would be shattered, pissed off because now it would seem that the lifestyle that I'd subconsciously created in order to seek what I needed, had actually achieved nothing. If my size really had no effect on those around me, my losing weight and starving myself had, for over seven years, been futile. A complete waste of miserable time. I couldn't believe that this might possibly be true.

As far as I was concerned, my anorexia had been the making of me. It determined everything that I did and every thought that I had, and willingly I had assumed the role that not eating had demanded. I was as much a part of my anorexia as it was of me. I was no longer an independent person. I was, by definition, anorexic. Finding it difficult to comprehend that anyone could possibly see me as anything else, I just couldn't believe that my weight did not affect how others viewed me. I was convinced that it did. Yet I had no evidence to either back up my claim, or to make any sense out of the uncertainty of not knowing what other people were thinking. One thing I did know, however, was that I needed to find out whether people did react differently towards me because of the anorexia or not. I'd never considered asking anybody this before, but I needed to now.

Afraid of uncovering the truth and losing my identity, tonight I felt huge.

November 30th, 1990

If becoming a nobody was one of my greatest fears, coping with time was another. Perhaps the greatest enemy of the depressed, time determined all else and prolonged hurting out of nothing. To me it was useless. A continuous passage of units, synchronised from one brain to the next and lacking all emotion. Unfaltering monotony with regard for no man, time the creator of boredom slowed everything down and screwed everything up. I hated it. I hated boredom too and days when I couldn't be bothered to do anything. And intelligence. Boredom seemed so pointless, intelligence so unkind. A constant test of patience, an unfair test of coping. In cruel partnership with time, calculating and destructive, boredom and intelligence allowed no mind to rest and certainly didn't mine.

Given today off from the hospital to allow for staff training, this morning I awoke to face the daunting prospect of three long and unstructured days ahead of me. An extended weekend break, a brief taste of how my life would be when I left hospital for the last time – I was on my own. Plagued by depressing serious thoughts which brought the future closer to home, with no idea how to occupy myself into coping, today I spent the day in bed and did not enjoy my independence. Feeling that I'd never enjoy anything ever again, I dreaded being on my own for good.

December 1st, 1990
World AIDS Day

Today I recalled reading somewhere that there were seventeen thousand more deaths caused by anorexia each year, in America alone, than there were deaths from AIDS world-wide up until the end of 1988.

December 3rd, 1990

Today I returned to St. Andrew's for my twelfth week of therapy. As usual the week kicked off with everyone declaring a personal aim to the group to be achieved by the end of the week. Still confused about whether people perceived me differently because of my anorexia or not, I announced that it was my intention to begin finding out how others really did view me.

Ashamed to have to admit the truth to myself, talking with Katie today I felt sad upon realising that after all this time, my label had perhaps never been anything other than a comforting fantasy on my behalf. A romantic grasp for attention that had, I was beginning to see, maybe not worked. Probably having suspected the ineffectiveness of my behaviour from the day she'd first met me, instead of sharing my gloom and doom, Katie reacted with optimism. Acknowledging the significance of me beginning to doubt the social importance of my anorexia, turning my realisation around she provided me with an alternative perspective from which to judge my situation. By pointing out that she'd only ever observed people reacting positively towards me, assuming that my illness did not affect the behaviour of others, she suggested that it was me that people genuinely responded to and not the anorexia. Implying that I had always been the important factor in determining how others chose to perceive me, effectively Katie was casting the significance of my anorexia into the shadows.

Slowly starting to understand the implications of this, it suddenly struck me that if it was right that others hadn't or wouldn't like or care for me any less if I stopped being ill, there was no point in me being ill anymore. Of course, I still needed to determine how exactly everyone did view me and of course there were still risks attached, but even so, I think at that point I began to realise that I'd hit upon something that was really quite important.

Maybe I didn't need to be anorexic. Maybe people did genuinely like me and respond well to me – because of me and who I was – rather than the illness that I had. Maybe it didn't matter to my friends that I was anorexic and maybe they didn't need a reason to worry and care about me. Maybe they did that because they wanted to. Perhaps too they didn't feel that they 'had to' make me feel special and valued, maybe that came from choice as well. Maybe? Maybe not? I didn't know.

Feeling a little excited by the possibility that some of my fears might not be realised, I quickly came back down to earth when Katie brought up the subject of me leaving St. Andrew's. Having conveniently forgotten for a while that I was supposed to be working towards leaving hospital at the end of December, I answered honestly when I told her that I'd chosen not to think about leaving. I didn't feel ready to leave therapy just yet. Coming off laxatives and dealing with the feelings that that had thrown up at me, I felt had set me back a couple of weeks and now December seemed too soon. Recognising that I was still making considerable progress, Katie agreed that I might benefit from attending therapy beyond my original target date and suggested that I should work towards leaving St. Andrew's on January 11th instead.

December 6th, 1990

Today when Katie weighed me, I weighed seven stone and ten pounds. Somehow in seeing a significant difference between seven-stone-ten and the seven-stone-thirteen that I'd been the previous week, instead of feeling distressed at remaining some way above my original weight, this morning I felt strangely contented. It was weird. I could see clearly that the scales were registering seven-stone-ten and yet for some reason I no longer felt fat. Perhaps it was just temporary relief at finally seeing myself stabilise, perhaps not. I couldn't for the life of me begin to understand why, when previously I'd felt huge at just over seven stone, now weighing considerably more, I should suddenly feel acceptable, but I did.

Describing this shift in my thinking during the small group session today, I'm pretty sure that at least three other people in the room had seriously doubted that this could be possible. Amazed that I should ever have come to a point of feeling OK about my weight, I couldn't explain what had happened but I felt good. Marking the end of what had probably been the worst two weeks of my life, I couldn't quite believe what I'd managed to achieve. Giving up laxatives had been the hardest thing that I'd ever attempted to do. For over a fortnight my feelings and thoughts had pushed me to my limits and beaten everything out of me, but now I was eating more or less what I had been before and at last my body had stabilised.

Bloody hell I'd done it. Yes, OK, I'd gained a bit of weight but I'd managed to stay with it and now I felt fine. My body, my head, everything - felt fine. I didn't feel suicidal anymore, I wasn't craving food or thinking about it constantly, hell I wasn't even depressed anymore. Yes. I'd done it, I'd reached the point everyone told me I would. They hadn't lied and I'd made it happen. I'd reached my impossible and I couldn't believe it.

December 10th, 1990

Realising that I still hadn't done anything about finding out how other people reacted towards me regarding my anorexia and still sensing this to be important, I promised the group that I'd definitely do something about it this week.

Feeling closer to not being anorexic than I had done before, tonight whilst thinking of my friends, I panicked a little and got quite upset. Although I was slowly coming round to the idea that my illness had not in any way made me special to anyone, I still couldn't wholeheartedly believe that friends would continue to care about me if I became fully well again. Feeling really scared that I would lose everyone's concern, whilst half of me wanted nothing more than to leave my anorectic ways behind me, I could sense very strongly that the rest of me didn't.

Whether I'd admitted it to myself or not, I'd known for a long time that I was selfishly afraid of not being anorexic anymore. Scared, despite what everyone said, that people would stop thinking and caring about me if I was no longer anorexic, ironically now I also dreaded being well enough to have to leave St. Andrew's. As happily established within the hospital's friendly and lively caring environment as I had been at sixth form, leaving was the last thing that I wanted to do. Reminding me all too well of when my sixth form days had ended, as had happened then, I faced and feared losing everything that had become important to me. I didn't want again to be separated from friends I didn't want to be separated from. I didn't want to lose the fun, laughter and chaos that kept my mind sane. I'd miss the banter at coffee time, the friendship that had kept me going, the good times and the bad. I'd miss the trust and respect that had held us all together, the acceptance and the compassion. I'd miss the empathy and understanding that had held me together and I'd miss not having every reason for getting up in the morning. Most of all, I'd miss belonging to a set of people who had created of me so much out of so little.

I'd gained an incredible amount from attending the day hospital and now I had so much to lose. That was how I felt anyway.

December 14th, 1990

This morning a Christmas card arrived at the hospital addressed 'To The People Who Scare The Workmen'. Sent by a fellow client shortly after he'd left St. Andrew's, as no doubt intended, this completely appealed to my nutty little nature and left me smiling again.

Smiling apart however, with the end of the week group meeting rapidly approaching, as was usual for a Friday, I found myself desperately trying to think of something to say which would suggest, without lying, that I'd spent time working upon what I'd intended for the week, when I hadn't. Failing miserably (which had also become the norm) and feeling more than a little guilty at having procrastinated yet again, with literally five minutes to spare, I asked those sitting drinking coffee around me for honest feedback as to how they viewed me now; how they had viewed me before I'd gained weight from giving up laxatives; and how they would view me if I was no longer anorexic.

Feeling uncomfortable and afraid of hearing responses that I didn't want to hear, in fact I was pleasantly surprised. For a start, despite me gaining almost a stone in weight, nobody had apparently noticed any change in my size. Reinforcing this observation, one of the girls from my small group said that she'd half wondered whether I'd been exaggerating about how much weight I'd gained, because she couldn't believe that I'd gained more than a few pounds. She admitted that my face had looked swollen and puffy for a few days after I'd given the laxatives up, but apart from that she'd noticed absolutely no difference in me. Another client told me that I'd never looked fat and pointed out that even when I was at my biggest after gaining the fluid, I'd still looked thin.

Furthermore, with respect to me not being anorexic anymore, from those comments that I received, instead of feeling that people would have reason to lose interest in me I was actually left feeling the opposite. Asserting that my personality was far more important to others than my appearance could ever be, whilst one of the nurses told me how pleased he'd be to see me well again, someone else pointed out that far from thinking less of me, those who knew me really well would probably admire and think more of me for fighting to become well again.

Confirming that my weight status probably never had coloured anyone else's perception of me, the above comments also suggested that I might have more to gain from defeating my anorexia than I'd ever imagined. Obsessed with thinking of recovery purely in terms of loss, it had never occurred to me to think instead of what I might gain. Far too narrow minded for my own good, rather than safeguarding a few needs, I realised that negative thinking of this order had probably denied me far more. Certainly it had hindered my progress.

Appreciating only too well why I'd come to fear no longer being anorexic, turning everything around for a moment, I pictured myself worthy of receiving positive attention for a change and suddenly I began to see everything differently. I wanted to gain respect but I wanted to earn it. I wanted my efforts to be recognised for what they were, and I wanted to be noticed for good reasons and not bad. I wanted to succeed and to be seen to be successful. I wanted to shock and surprise and bring pleasure to those who had seen me at my lowest. I wanted to stand out from the crowd. I wanted to be an achiever, a failed failure. I wanted to rid myself of self-deception and to be proud of something that I'd done.

Above all, I wanted to prove to myself – more than anybody else – that anorexia was defeatable.

December 18th, 1990

If lifelessness had shrouded my existence, I'd been oblivious to it until today. Completely useless this afternoon, whilst staring into the expressionless gaze of another I feared having to comprehend its very meaning and I could do nothing.

Having gone out at the weekend and enjoyed herself, one of my small group members, another anorectic, was now on hunger strike, refusing to either eat or drink. Visibly weak, and barely able to hang onto the chair beneath her, like the very world around her I could almost see her slipping away before me. With pained insight I knew where she was coming from and I wanted to stop her in her tracks, but I couldn't. She was unreachable. Lost and bewildered. But an arm's reach away and yet distanced beyond hope. Watching the destruction of an infatuated mind, I saw hopelessness far deeper than ever before and it hurt. She wasn't even drinking water and she was so stubborn. She scared me. Like thrashing on a door and getting no response, I tried to break her but my efforts just bounced back. An unrewarding iciness which echoed nothing other than death and I couldn't escape it. But nothing and no man could make her eat.

Desperate to shake her, I found myself repeating to her everything that everyone had said to me over the years, but nothing of what I said made sense. At least to me it never had done before, but now I was seeing things differently. Whereas once I'd been lost within her frightening irrationality, now I could see beyond it but my understanding was useless. In fact it wasn't 'understanding' because I didn't understand. I couldn't understand why she wouldn't eat. She was so thin and so frail, and water was so harmless. Why? Of all people I should have been able to reach her and I tried. I tried everything, Everything that I had, everything I could think of – but nothing. Death was laughing me in the face and I could do nothing to stop it.

Disturbed into viewing my own situation through the eyes of everybody else, in recognising my own stubbornness and determination to remain unwell, I felt both guilty and sad. I was more than aware of what being anorexic had done to me and now finally I was aware too of what it had done to those around me, helpless to do anything just as I was now. Determined to change all of that, becoming well again suddenly had new meaning. I wanted to leave my anorexia behind me. I wanted nothing more to do with it. I wanted the satisfaction of beating it into submission and I wanted to be in control of my life again. I wanted to forget all about lifelessness and I wanted never again to encounter it in either myself or anybody else.

I wanted many things. None were impossible. All I had to do was let go of the last few strands of false security, which up until now I'd been creating around me. I didn't need them or my anorexia anymore. I knew that there had to be a better life out there somewhere, waiting. I just had to believe that I could cope without not eating.

December 20th, 1990

With Christmas rapidly approaching, I was worried about having to cope away from the hospital for ten days, and I discussed my anxieties with Katie. I couldn't quite work out what was upsetting me but I could sense that I was apprehensive about something. In trying to identify the cause of this apparent uncertainty (and having rejected a number of possibilities) I eventually came to the conclusion that I was afraid of resorting back to my old ways of being completely unassertive whilst at home.

Having never been anything other than passive at home, being assertive there was something that I'd never encountered before. Afraid of saying or doing anything that might upset my parents, I was the first to admit that I found it difficult being myself at home. Scared that my best could never be good enough, home was the place where I tried hardest to please everyone. Terrified of those around me engaging in conflict, whether peace was threatened or not, home was also the place where I did everything within my power to keep conflict at bay by trying to keep everybody happy. Holding back any thoughts that I considered to be negative, like the rest of my family, at home I never voiced unpleasant comments. I never expressed how I was feeling. I never asked for my needs to be met. I never felt able to be angry and I never really knew what anyone else was thinking or feeling. Leaving everything to guess work, at home I'd neglect personal rights, needs and responsibilities and all around me I'd breed a perfect atmosphere for non-communication. With time I'd feel misunderstood and disillusioned, and always I'd lose peace with myself.

Not at all sure of whether I'd ever be able to assert myself at home, Katie suggested today that I might use the Christmas break to stand back and work out how best I might try to be assertive there. Seeing this as an ideal excuse for justifiably avoiding situations in which I felt threatened, I thought this a good idea and secretly decided to implement it whenever it suited me.

December 21st, 1990

In light-hearted mode and courtesy of the Health Authority, today the staff organised a buffet lunch and threw a Christmas party for us all. Preparing me for more of what was to come, I quite surprised myself by enjoying today.

If Christmas was always awful it was precisely because I always 'arranged' it to be so. I didn't want to not enjoy myself and like everyone else I wanted to have a good time, but I suppose in many ways I'd always differed in that I didn't really know how to enjoy myself. Deciding that this was going to change, this evening I drove home to Stockton determined not only to analyse my behaviour but also to make the most of Christmas.

Partly prepared for the holiday, in terms of responding to unknown awkward situations, I felt better for knowing that I'd always have three unchanging response options. Having analysed a given situation, I could either:

1) do nothing
2) accept that whatever was beyond my responsibility; or
3) assert myself in an attempt to facilitate beneficial change.

Knowing which of the three I wanted to move away from, I viewed the holiday ahead more as a challenge than anything else. Whether I enjoyed myself or not, I realised, was within my power. I had nothing to lose and everything to gain from becoming more effective at home. That said however, I still had to learn how to be assertive at home and I didn't think for one minute that it would be easy.

Feeling the need to break myself in gently, I decided that I would try to *think* assertively over Christmas. Allowing myself the option of not having to follow thoughts with assertive actions, strangely, just by making that decision I felt stronger. Regardless of what the holiday had in store for me, at the end of the day I'd always have a choice and that choice would always be mine. That was the important thing.

Arriving home tonight I only just managed to beat Roger to Stockton. Having driven down from Dundee, he walked up the drive and knocked on our door about four minutes after I got home. Lifting me from the doorstep and threatening to drop me bum first in the paw printed mud at the foot of the drive, within seconds of seeing him again I felt reassured that I was going to have a good holiday.

December 24th, 1990

I suppose there comes a time in the life of every good intention when it has to falter and I guess that time for mine was today. I couldn't understand why I should feel huge this morning when I weighed the same as I had done yesterday and had felt fine then, but I did and I couldn't stand it.

Feeling fatter than I had done in ages, for some reason this morning the size of my chest completely disturbed me. It seemed ridiculous, beyond a joke, I hated it and I'd had enough. Desperately needing to distance myself from the irrationality it brought, today I freaked whilst having a shower and completely lost it. Totally out of control I ripped at my chest with my nails and shredded and shredded at the skin. Well and truly off my head I just couldn't stop. I didn't know why I'd woken up feeling fat again and I didn't know why exactly I was laying into myself so compulsively, but I couldn't help it. The tearing was too automatic and too determined for me to do anything to halt it. Vicious and uncaring, the strength with which my hands moved told me that I needed something but I didn't know what or why. All I saw were furious bruised scratches and raised welts with stinging lines of purple red, raw exhaustion and blood beneath my nails. I was a mess. Blocking anything of any sense, whatever had upset me and left me feeling fat, was now gone. Shredded confusion diffused once more. My body had become taken over by a mind that didn't know what was happening and that freaked me all the more. Again self-harming had worked.

Despising myself for being me, today I wanted someone else to live my life for me. Translated into rational logic, although I couldn't pin-point any incident in particular, tonight I guessed that somewhere along the line I probably hadn't been as assertive as I'd needed to be and what had gone unsaid I'd now acted out. Unidentified anger and frustration hidden no longer, my neglected responsibilities were painfully clear again.

December 25th, 1990
Today passed and I coped, calmed into some non-reactive mode and busied into not thinking.

December 29th, 1990
Talking with Roger this afternoon, he told me that he'd noticed a lot of positive changes in me. In general, he felt I'd become more confident, less stressed, a lot happier and much more in control of everything going on around me.

With our friends, he'd seen me behave in ways that I'd never done before and he'd seen me enjoy myself genuinely. He'd noticed me challenge both himself and others during discussions. He'd heard me disagree with other people's views and he'd witnessed me express ideas, views and opinions that again, he'd not seen me do before. He'd watched me take responsibility for deciding and expressing what I did and did not want to do. He'd heard me say 'no' to things

I didn't think I'd enjoy and he said that he'd got a real kick from watching my face when other people had responded well to the alternative suggestions that I'd made.

He also said how much better he felt our relationship was. He told me that he really felt he was getting to know the real me and that all the time, he was liking what he saw and heard more and more. Feeling that I was much more relaxed and laid back with him, he said that he felt closer to me than ever before and that he felt that I was closer to him too. No longer as unaware of his feelings as I had been, he felt that I was more responsive towards him, and said that he felt better appreciated and understood. He told me that he felt things between us were more equal, that I was less defensive and that he was less scared of speaking his mind for fear of upsetting me. He felt that he could now really talk to me and pointed out how pleased he was that I now spoke up about things that upset me, instead of keeping them to myself. He told me that he felt that my anorexia was no longer dominating me and said he felt the two of us were much less restricted by it.

Telling me that he loved me more than ever, he told me again how proud he was of all that I'd achieved and, hugging me tightly, finally he just said how lovely it was to see me really living and enjoying life again.

December 30th, 1990

Today there were lots of tears shed over a few drops of spilt Domestos and I had only myself to blame. I hadn't told my parents that I'd stopped abusing laxatives, mainly because once stopped I just wanted to forget about the whole affair without it ever rearing its ugly head again. I'd also assumed that since my parents had been aware of me using them, now they would likewise be aware that I'd stopped. Apparently not so.

This afternoon, on finding one of the loos blocked at home, and fearing that conclusions involving me would automatically be jumped at, I attempted to un-block the bloody thing. In the process of doing so, I managed accidentally to spill a few drops of the aforementioned Domestos on the bathroom carpet. It left a small, decolourised blotch, to mark with vigour the guilt of what had after all been a

181

good if face saving deed, and my mum was not happy. In fact she was livid. Furious that the carpet was damaged and furious with me, I was left in no doubt that once again my integrity was being watched. I could blame nobody but myself for that and I could understand why my mum was angry, but I still felt gutted by her reaction and I couldn't help but feel angry too. Angry at being accused unfairly of as good as deliberately ruining the carpet, when clearly the spillage had been accidental. Angry with myself for having created such a situation in the first place, and angry at being drawn into conflict completely against my wishes.

I could not remember the last time that anyone had been so annoyed at something that I'd done. Nor could I recall ever having felt as angry as I did and that I saw to be immensely important. My feelings had been those of anger, real anger. True emotion justifiably identified and unmasked. I hadn't felt fat, I'd just felt anger. A healthy step forward.

January 1st, 1991

'All is quiet on New Year's Day,
A world in white gets underway.'

'New Year's Day', U2

My New Year's resolution for 1991 was to spend the time that previously I'd wasted in trying to destroy myself, looking after myself instead.

January 2nd, 1991
Returning to the hospital, today I reflected upon what I felt I'd achieved whilst at home. Apart from the benefits of seeing Roger and sharing the progress that he'd seen me make, I felt as though I'd learnt a great deal.

Having managed to distance myself from much of what had been going on around me, the holiday had brought with it greater understanding. I'd come to see home in its true light and I now no longer perceived it to be the falsely idyllic place that I had once done. Hitting home to me how difficult I found it to communicate on a deeper than everyday level with my family, I'd realised how unassertive I was. I'd noticed that there was a lot of pent-up tension at home and no one to release it, and I'd felt the atmosphere become strained and tense whenever I was around. Whereas arguments had always given way to an unhealthy silence, this time at home I'd watched everyone in my family avoid conflict and I'd realised that I had a lot to do with it. Unaware previously that I was the one who cast the egg shells, now I could see that it was true. Once cast however, I wasn't the only one tiptoeing by for fear of upsetting the balance and causing friction. In the same way that I'd always been too scared of speaking my mind and being honest about feelings, so too were my family for fear of upsetting me. Bringing home more than a few home truths, I'd become aware of some of the effects that my behaviour had been having upon my family. If a little difficult to accept, I'd seen from a fresh angle a number of my own behaviours that I didn't particularly like and I could see that I still had much to work upon.

That said however, whereas previously the focus of my thoughts and feelings had tended always towards food and personal size, perhaps for the first time, this emphasis had shifted. Bringing new awareness of real emotions to mind, by getting through the Domestos stress situation without feeling fat, I realised that I'd set myself an important precedent. Capable of facing up to difficulties without a 'feeling fat' escape mechanism, I'd proved to myself that I'd reached a point of coping which no longer depended upon me blotting everything out behind perceived fatness.

January 4th, 1991

This evening whilst flicking back over old photographs, for the first time I noticed just how thin I'd been. It was really strange. I must have looked at the same photographs previously, on countless occasions and yet never had I recognised how weak and feeble and pale I'd been. But if that was weird, looking in the mirror was even more so. Despite now accepting that I had once looked thin and perhaps even ill, I still for the life of me could not determine how I looked now. I honestly couldn't tell whether I was fat or not, and yet somehow it just didn't seem important anymore.

January 6th, 1991

Still very uneasy about the issue of conflict, this afternoon I encountered it again. Having returned to Stockton to spend time with Roger before he returned to Dundee, I found myself caught up in a rare family disagreement. Unlike the day of the Domestos, today the row taking place had absolutely nothing to do with me. Where in the past I'd have been tempted to bring an end to the shouting by automatically taking the blame both for causing, and the responsibility for ending, family conflict, today I didn't. Aware that I was not in any way to blame for the angry words which were being exchanged, by standing back from the situation I managed to judge and accept that I was in no way responsible for what was being said. I also realised that I had neither right nor reason to take on board anyone else's ill feelings.

I still felt quite upset but instead of blowing everything out of all proportion and worrying myself stupid and fat in the process, I took it upon myself just to walk away and to let the situation sort itself out. In fact I drove back to York and much to my amazement, I discovered that by simply distancing myself from that which hadn't had anything to do with me in the first place, I was quickly able to forget about the whole incident. An achievement which a few months ago I wouldn't even have been able to think about attempting, again I'd proved to myself that awkward situations did not have to get the better of me. I had a brain and I was perfectly capable of coping on my own. All I had to do was gear my mind into thinking assertively.

Rights, needs and responsibilities: suddenly in seeing them as the answer to everything, I realised that if I could take care of them, they would take care of me.

January 7th, 1991

Entering my last week at St. Andrew's today I had mixed feelings. With only five days left to prepare myself for leaving and rejoining the big bad world, it wasn't going to be long before I was on my own again. Determined to get the most out of my last few days with everyone at St. Andrew's, I decided not to dwell on the leaving side of things. That would be sad enough when it happened. Looking forward instead, I felt I'd benefit more from identifying (and preparing myself for) potential difficulties I could meet once I'd left the hospital.

Fearing that boredom could be my greatest cause of downfall, I chose for my last intention to concentrate on finding ways of preventing myself from becoming bored once I left. I knew that I'd face having a hell of a lot of unstructured time on my hands and I knew that if I wasn't careful I could quite easily find myself back at square one.

Feeling bright and optimistic about the future, today as I discussed possible intentions for the months ahead, I realised that unlike before when I hadn't been bothered to do anything, now there were plenty of things that I really wanted to do. I wanted to spend time with Roger in Dundee. I wanted to write. I wanted to catch up properly with friends both within York and without. I wanted to drink alcohol again and finish my degree. I wanted to keep in touch with the friends I'd made at St. Andrew's and I wanted, perhaps more than anything, to give back some of what had been given to me.

Ahead of me I had the ideal opportunity to do whatever I wanted and it felt good. As hard as I tried I couldn't feel that I'd ever be bored again and although I would have loved to remain part of St. Andrew's forever, I could sense that part of me was itching to go. Excited, I was ready for the off. I wanted to get out and face the world again, I wanted to boast my successes and I wanted everyone to know that I'd beaten anorexia.

January 8th, 1991

Today I took part in my last drama session. Looking again towards the future, this afternoon I was struck by just how positive my thoughts were. Trying to think myself into situations I'd find difficult to handle, I found myself totally unable to imagine things going wrong. I tried to imagine myself all alone in my room, depressed and lonely and not wanting to do anything other than stay in bed. I tried to think my way back to the feelings of panic that controlled everything when I felt fat. I tried to picture myself going off my head with frustration and flying into a frenzy which I couldn't control. And I tried to imagine what it would be like to spend years wishing time away and wanting to be dead, as I had once done. But I couldn't.

With images and a past that no longer made sense to me, I realised that I knew too many people in too many places to ever justify revisiting the place I'd fought so hard to leave behind.

Determined not to let myself or anybody else down again, what surprised me most about this thinking was that it came to me automatically. Yielding out of nowhere an attitude far removed from a past that had, up until now, obscured the future behind tarnished and reluctant hopes, now my hopes were alive. Life made sense again and my destiny, secured by confidence, was mine. In fact the future from now on I felt very much to be mine, and nothing, I decided, would get the better of me again. Not if I could help it anyway.

January 11th, 1991

And so, perhaps all too quickly my last day at St. Andrew's finally dawned. A beautiful day with blue skies edged in tree broken frost. A day which I'd believed would never come.

No longer trapped within a past of non-communication and no longer wrapped up in a life which was not to be, at long last I'd done it. I'd beaten my anorexia. Mesmerised by feelings of achievement and pride, where once my imagination had haunted my dreams and led me astray, now no more. Having caused my darkness to be melted and my memories to be dusted with people I'd never forget, St. Andrew's had done wonders for me and I'd been given, completely, the sudden sense of liberty that I'd briefly encountered in October. No longer fixed with sadness or restricted by myself, my potential had come back to me and set my world to rest. Clear and decisive, I knew what I wanted out of life and I felt ready to go out and achieve what I never had before.

'I used to think that the day would never come,
I'd see the light in the shade of the morning sun.
My morning sun is a drug that brings me near,
To the childhood I lost replaced by fear.'

'True Faith', New Order

No longer wilting and no longer afraid of the sun, as I said my good-byes and hugged those around me, I felt a little sad at knowing that I'd not see them all together again, but more than anything I felt proud. After seven years of believing that anorexia was not defeatable, I'd proven that it was. I'd made my impossible happen and I just had to look at the smiles on the faces of those seeing me well again, to know that I was going to enjoy not being anorexic.

Peace of mind, caring, friends and a past now understood – now I really did have everything. Hugging me tightly on the doorstep, Katie told me that she'd never seen me looking so well. It was to her, Roger and a few others, that I owed almost everything.

PART FOUR

Beyond Therapy

January 2000

After leaving St. Andrew's in the January of 1991, I remained in York where I spent eight months writing before returning to college. Having completed my degree, I left York in the summer of 1993 and moved up to Dundee to live with Roger, whilst he finished his studies. In the spring of 1995 Roger and I moved down to London where we lived for eighteen months, before settling in Hertfordshire. Between 1995 and 1997 I studied for a diploma in counselling. Having decided to specialise in eating disorders, since 1996 I have worked as a counsellor in a specialist eating disorder unit and for a national charity. About to move to Cambridgeshire, I will be able to provide specialist eating disorder counselling to clients living within the Cambridgeshire region.

Over the nine years that have passed since I was discharged from therapy, I have remained fit and healthy and free from anorexia. When I left St. Andrew's I weighed more or less the target weight for my height, and since then my weight has largely remained stable. Initially I did gain a little weight as I experimented with eating more but, once I'd worked out how much I needed to eat to stop myself from either gaining or losing weight, I very quickly stabilised again.

When I first left therapy, I decided to try eating what I wanted when I wanted it. Despite being a little repetitive and maybe restrictive in terms of the types of foods eaten, I found that this approach to eating worked well for me and I still use it today. Occasionally I go through phases of craving the same meal over and over again and I do tend to eat a lot of chocolate but, as long as my weight remains stable, the content of my diet really doesn't bother me. After years of denying my body so many different kinds of foods, I feel now that the cravings I get for certain tastes are probably quite natural.

Initially as I began allowing myself to eat freely foods that previously I'd restricted, I was worried that I wouldn't be able to stop myself bingeing once I'd got a taste again for foods that I really enjoyed. I was also scared that I might fall full length into bulimia, but I found that for me this didn't happen. Probably because I was allowing myself to eat sufficient amounts of the foods I craved, regularly and often (i.e. in snack proportions rather than 'normal' meals) I didn't feel the urge to binge. I think realising that I could more or less eat what I wanted without needing to worry about my weight, also helped.

Certainly reaching this point (something I thought I'd never do) has helped to keep me happy and free from the depression that controlled me when I was anorexic. That said however, during the last nine years there have been a couple of times when I've felt a little down. Usually reflecting a natural response to something difficult that I've come up against, or a time when I've felt I wasn't achieving something, whenever this has happened I've managed to bounce back pretty easily and usually eating hasn't been an issue.

There has been only one occasion since I left St. Andrew's when eating has become an issue and I've felt at risk of slipping back again. At the beginning of my final year at college, in the autumn of 1992, I spent eight weeks on teaching practice in a York school, hating every minute of it. Working alongside an experienced teacher who clearly had little regard for student teachers and equally clearly didn't like me, for two months I found myself feeling completely trapped again. Scared that I might fail the practice (and with it my degree) if I spoke up about conditions that had become unbearable, instead of being assertive, for eight weeks I chose to handle unreasonable situation after situation passively and I really suffered for it. Feeling powerless and convinced that I was going to fail the practice, by the end of my time at the school I felt as though I'd achieved nothing. My self-esteem had tumbled, I'd become extremely depressed and my weight had started to fall again. I snapped out of the not eating as soon as I completed (and passed) teaching practice, and I'm convinced now that had I behaved assertively throughout its duration, I wouldn't have become depressed and I wouldn't have needed to focus upon restricting my eating in order to cope.

Aware already of the role that assertiveness had played in enabling me to recover from anorexia, it wasn't until I reflected back over what I'd experienced as soon as I'd slipped back in to behaving passively, that I really began to appreciate what developing assertiveness had done for me. I'm now of the opinion that it was varying levels of assertiveness which influenced the development of, maintenance of and success of recovery from, my anorexia. (The diagram overleaf attempts to explain the rationale behind this thinking.)

Suspecting that the development of assertiveness might hold the key to recovery for most (if not all) eating disordered people, during the last four years I have based much of my counselling practice upon the assertiveness-based therapy that I received at St. Andrew's. Confirming my ideas about the role of increased assertiveness in the recovery from eating disorders, throughout this time I have been encouraged to see other clients make similar progress to that which I had.

Offering promising implications for the future, if it can be shown that *lack* of assertiveness leads people *into* disordered eating whilst the *development* of assertiveness leads people *out* of it, it strikes me that assertiveness training may hold the answer to improving the success of eating disorder treatment programs in this country. Furthermore, if the development of assertiveness can be shown to reduce vulnerability to the development of depressive illnesses such as anorexia and bulimia, it would seem to me that assertiveness training might also hold interesting implications regarding the *prevention* of eating disorders. With this in mind, whilst in the short term I wish to continue working in clinical practice, in the longer term, I would very much like to work towards the possible prevention of eating disorders (and other depressive illnesses), by investigating whether benefits might be gained through incorporating assertiveness training into mainstream education.

RESULTING IN

THE DEVELOPMENT OF:

- Effective communication behaviours
- Strengthened and fulfilling relationships
- Personal abilities, competencies, and achievements
- Personal satisfaction and contentment
- The ability of an individual to function effectively and to generate health, happiness and success for self, without need for coping mechanism.

RESULTING IN

THE INCREASED VULNERABILITY OF THE INDIVIDUAL TO THE DEVELOPMENT OF MALADAPTIVE BEHAVIOURS ARISING FROM PASSIVITY &/OR AGGRESSION, AND THE NEED FOR COPING MECHANISMS SUCH AS:

- Depression
- Phobias
- Alcohol/Drug Dependency
- Bullying Behaviours
- Delinquency
- Deviation into crime
- EATING DISORDERS

RESULTING IN

The Role of Assertiveness in the Development, Maintenance, Conquering and Prevention of Eating Disorders.

SELF ESTEEM

LEADING TO

INFLUENCES

LEADING TO

ASSERTIVENESS

HIGH LEVELS OF ASSERTIVENESS AND SELF ESTEEM

Ability to view self as an equal, to stand up for and to satisfy personal rights and needs;
Ability to deal with responsibilities appropriately;
Ability to deal with conflict &/or negative feelings healthily;
Abilities to make decisions, to take control of self, and to influence others positively;
Confidence in one's self and abilities;
Feelings of equality, value, worth, respect and liking directed by self and others towards the self;
Ability to achieve aspirations, goals, personal potentials;
Empowerment, direction, and hope for the future;
Reduced personal stress levels;
No need for further coping mechanism.

LOW LEVELS OF ASSERTIVENESS AND SELF ESTEEM

Inability to view self as an equal, to stand up for and to satisfy personal rights and needs;
Inability to deal with responsibilities appropriately;
Inability to deal with conflict &/or negative feelings (tendency to turn anger inwards or misdirect it towards others);
Inability to say 'no', to make decisions or to ask for wants;
Inability to control/influence situations, self and others effectively;
Inability to form fulfilling relationships with others;
Exploitation and manipulation of by others (real or perceived);
Loss of direction and identity;
Feelings of worthlessness, valuelessness, isolation, alienation, inferiority, frustration, and powerlessness;
Self hatred, fear, hopelessness etc.;
Increased personal stress levels;
The need for a coping mechanism.

Regrets

I have few regrets concerning the fact that I developed anorexia as I believe now that for me, at the time, developing some form of coping mechanism had become necessary. Given that I did become anorexic however, there are a few things concerning the management of my illness that I personally regret not having handled differently at the time.

Firstly, I very much regret not having asked for help much earlier than I did. Had I taken the care to listen to what friends had been saying for years and had I decided to see a doctor instead of just ignoring give away signs, I seriously doubt that my anorexia would have lasted as long as it did. Another thing that I regret is the fact that I failed completely to recognise the severity of either my disordered eating or depressed state of mind. Convinced for some reason that my fears around eating and weight and my depressed mood were not 'bad enough' to be considered a 'real' problem, I wish now that I'd not added to my problems by negating the constant unhappiness that all too quickly became the norm for me.

I also deeply regret ever having used and abused laxatives. Aware now of how cunning the body can be at grabbing those food stuffs it requires, especially in the face of adversity, with hindsight I realise that my experimentation with laxatives was completely futile. Falling into the dependency trap of laxative abuse was probably the easiest mistake I made during my anorexia. It was also probably the most stupid thing I did and it could quite easily have been the most costly. Laxatives *do not* aid weight loss. In terms of shifting calories they are completely ineffective. With respect to screwing up an already miserable existence however, they are anything but effective and I still feel pretty angry that I didn't allow myself to listen to logic and reason, before I introduced my system to its first miserable dose.

Finally, although as I have already stated, I do not regret the fact that I became anorexic, I do very much regret the fact that my becoming anorexic was not prevented when I believe now that it could have been. Had I been taught to think and behave assertively and had I as a result of such learning developed those skills necessary to live a happy and healthy life, I don't think that my anorexia would have been necessary.

Self-Help Ideas, Strategies and Exercises

Having outlined the learning which enabled me to recover from anorexia in the earlier parts of this book, in this section I would like to present some of the strategies, exercises and ways of thinking which helped me develop the skills I needed. Concentrating upon those strategies and techniques behind the thinking skills responsible for my recovery, I include also a number of strategies that other clients have found useful when addressing frequently encountered issues and difficulties.

The Eating Disorders Association is an excellent source of support and offers advice on how to access specialist treatment and therapy. They are contactable at:

The Eating Disorders Association
First Floor
Wensum House
103 Prince of Wales Road
Norwich
Norfolk
NR1 1DW

Helpline: 01603 621 414 (Mon - Fri, 9 a.m - 6.30 p.m)
Youthline (18 year olds and under): 01603 765 050
(Mon - Fri, 4 p.m - 6 p.m)
Admin. line: 01603 619 090
e-mail: info@edauk.com
website: www.edauk.com

Helpful Ways of Thinking About:

Rights

A fundamental aspect of healthy human behaviour centres around the understanding that everybody has rights, and that everybody is entitled to have their rights recognised and respected. Terrified of being 'selfish' and therefore 'disliked', all too readily eating disordered people will recognise, respect and automatically protect the rights of others. Typically they will fail to even recognise that they themselves have rights and all too often their personal rights become negated and neglected. Resulting in low self-esteem and feelings of worthlessness and powerlessness, it is often the inability of the individual to think of and to treat him/herself as an equal, that plays a key role in keeping him/her anchored within the eating disordered state. In trying to break free from the confines of any eating disorder and attain sustained recovery, it is of fundamental importance that the individual learns to *recognise*, *appreciate* and *own* personal rights, and with time he/she must learn to respect and protect them.

I found it helpful, particularly in times of stress, to keep reminding myself of the following rights charter:

> 'I have the right to be treated with respect as an equal human being.
>
> I have the right to acknowledge my needs as being equal to those of others.
>
> I have the right to express my opinions, thoughts and feelings.
>
> I have the right to make mistakes.
>
> I have the right to choose not to take responsibility for other people.
>
> I have the right to be me without being dependent on the approval of others.'

(*Assertiveness: A Practical Approach*, p.11, Stephanie Holland and Clare Ward, Winslow Press, 1990)

Needs

In the same way that everybody has rights which need to be recognised and respected, so too does everybody have personal needs which also need to be recognised and respected. Totally different to 'wants', 'needs' by definition are essential pre-requisites to personal well-being and, whether those needs are emotional, physical, enjoyment, safety etc., everybody deserves equally to have their needs satisfied. Eating disordered people, usually having learnt at some stage to unhealthily associate having needs met with being 'selfish', 'greedy', 'dissatisfied', or 'bad', often find the concept of having personal needs met extremely uncomfortable and difficult to deal with.

Declaring personal needs and having them met does not mean that you are being 'selfish' or 'unreasonable', or behaving in any way so as to make others think badly of you. There is nothing to be gained from negating and neglecting personal needs, since effectively all this does is feed the control assumed by the eating disorder, whilst removing further control from the individual. Learning how to identify and declare needs and to depend upon both the self and others to have personal needs met, is an essential part of recovery from any eating disorder.

I found it useful at times when I was struggling, to think of each new need that I learnt to recognise and have satisfied, as one less need to fuel my dependence upon my anorexia.

Responsibilities

In order to function healthily, individuals need to take appropriate responsibility for their own thoughts, feelings and behaviours. Ensuring that the rights and needs of both the self and others are respected equally, appropriate responsibility prevents the unfair treatment of others and protects the self from the damaging effects of inappropriate negative feelings including self-blame, guilt, and regret. Controlled by fear and the need 'to keep everyone else happy', eating disordered people often fall into the dual trap of avoiding personal responsibilities whilst taking on responsibilities belonging to others.

Having done this myself for years, I find it helpful before responding to a given situation, to separate responsibilities into categories of those belonging to me and those belonging to someone else. In order to protect the rights and needs of both myself and others, I choose now only to take responsibility for my own thoughts, feelings and behaviours. How other people choose to think, feel and behave is *their* responsibility. If, for example, somebody chooses to allow something I have said or done to anger or upset them, I recognise now that their choice of reaction is their responsibility. If I have behaved unreasonably then it is my responsibility to apologise and make amends for my behaviour. I also have every reason to feel bad or guilty until the situation has been rectified or sorted out. If I can justify that my actions have been fair however, I accept now that responsibility for the other person's feelings, lies with that person and not me.

Likewise if, for example, I turn a request down and somebody else chooses to take my decision badly, any feelings of disappointment, anger or whatever, belong to them and it is not my place to feel responsible for their feelings. Everyone has the right (within reason) to say 'no' to things they don't want to do and if someone else chooses not to accept this, it is that person who is behaving unreasonably and not the person turning down the request.

Guilt

Of all the negative emotions, perhaps more than any other it is guilt that affects and indeed dictates the lifestyles of many anorectics and bulimics. Shaping decision-making and self-doubts, restricting healthy self-choices and behaviours, often those feelings of guilt experienced continually by individuals displaying eating disorders, develop as a direct result of them assuming inappropriate responsibility for other people's feelings.

Learning to dissociate yourself from the responsibility of feelings belonging to others and to accept that you have no right to feel guilty, or to blame yourself, for reactions or happenings occurring outside of your control, is an important part of liberating yourself from an eating disorder.

Being Assertive

Assertiveness is all about learning to take care of personal rights, needs and responsibilities, in such a way as to ensure that the rights and needs of the self are protected and satisfied, whilst ensuring that those of others are equally protected and satisfied. Assertiveness is not about being 'selfish', 'unreasonable', 'dominant', 'aggressive', or about individuals 'getting their own way all the time'. Based upon principles of equality, assertiveness involves individuals treating themselves and others as equals. It also depends upon people being totally responsible for their own thoughts, feelings and actions.

Although at times it can be extremely difficult to actually be assertive, developing assertiveness enables individuals to regain control of their lives and for this reason alone it can be extremely beneficial for anorectics and bulimics. Even getting into the habit of thinking assertively, whether assertive actions follow or not, can make a huge difference to an individual, perhaps feeling trapped by others or circumstances perceived to be uncontrollable.

Long before I'd gained the confidence to begin putting my thoughts into action, I often found it helpful (especially when feeling daunted by someone or a situation) to think to myself: 'he had no right to say that...' or 'I have the right to say 'no' if I want to, but (for whatever reason) just now I'm choosing to say 'yes''; or: 'he might be angry but I'm not going to blame myself or feel guilty, that's his responsibility, not mine...'

Selfishness

It is common for anorectics and bulimics, due to feelings of low self-esteem, to spend most of their time behaving so as to satisfy the needs of others, whilst neglecting or failing to recognise their own. Born of what can become a crippling fear of being perceived by others as 'selfish', it is often the eating disordered person's need to be 'liked by everyone' and their persistence to only engage in 'selfless' activities, which trap and prevent them from breaking free from the confines of their disordered eating.

Having broken free from a belief which convinced me for years that to be selfish was the worst thing that anybody could be, I now recognise that there are two kinds of selfishness: namely *unacceptable* selfishness and *necessary* selfishness. Unacceptable selfishness I consider to be those actions carried out by an individual to satisfy wants at the *avoidable expense* of another. Necessary selfishness by definition I consider to be those actions carried out by an individual, to satisfy needs *essential* to personal well-being and whose effects upon another (if at all) can be fully *justified*. Whilst I still believe that unacceptable selfishness is undesirable, since the well-being of the individual is ultimately the responsibility of the individual, I choose to believe also that necessary selfishness is an essential, and indeed a good component of healthy living.

Satisfying necessary self-needs is not a crime. To engage in necessary selfishness does not mean that you are a bad person or that people will begin to dislike you. Necessary selfishness demonstrates that you have the ability to be independent and to look after yourself; a quality that others might even begin to respect you for.

Self-Help Strategies

Stopping negative thoughts

Since it is usually the case that a whole chain of negative thoughts follow on from one negative thought, the key to stopping negative thought after negative thought, is to block the chain before it has a chance to develop. In order to do so, as soon as you become aware that you are thinking negatively:

1) Stop the thought in its tracks
Tell yourself something like: 'That's me being negative, I'm going to stop this.'

2) Challenge the negative thought
If you were thinking for example: 'I'm stupid and I deserve awful things to happen to me', take a minute to find one piece of evidence to suggest that the thought might not necessarily be true. You might choose to remind yourself that you're good at art or that you work well in your job and that you don't deserve awful things to happen to you because nobody deserves that.

3) Replace the negative thought with a positive one
Replace: 'I feel fat' with, for example, 'What can I do to take my mind off my feelings?'; 'I'm useless, I can't do anything' with 'I can choose to do whatever I like' and 'Today's awful and everything's going to go wrong' with 'Tomorrow might be better' etc.

4) Regardless of outcome, acknowledge the effort you are making to better yourself

5) Persevere with the above until the challenging itself becomes a new habit which replaces the habit that negative thinking had become
Depending upon the nature and frequency of negative thoughts experienced, it may take weeks or even months of continued effort to change your thinking completely – but with commitment it is possible to do so.

Confronting awkward people and/or situations effectively

Step one: Identifying the problem to be confronted
– What has upset you, what would you like to be different?
– Be specific: How exactly are you feeling just now?
     What exactly has happened to leave you feeling this way?
     Whose behaviour is responsible for your feelings?
     What was said/done, and in what way, by whom?
     When did this happen, where, has it happened before?
     What effect has this had upon you and why?

Step two: Deciding what you want to achieve from the confrontation
– What exactly would you like the desired outcome to be?
– Be specific. What would you like to: change?
     : be different?
     : happen more frequently?
     : not happen again?
     Would you like others to behave differently?
     What exactly would you like them to, or not to, say/do?
     When, where, how often would you like whatever?
     Would you like others to know how they have left you feeling?
     What precisely would you like to tell them?

Step three: Preparing what to say and do during the confrontation
– Decide where and when you wish the meeting to take place.
– Work out exactly what you want to say during the meeting.
– Prepare a 'stock phrase' which encapsulates clearly:
     a) what the problem is, and
     b) what you want to change.
– Try to anticipate how the person might react and prepare answers/
responses you will use if, for example, they
     : react angrily, shout or become aggressive
     : blame you, become defensive or deny
      responsibility for whatever

      : become upset and burst into tears

      : refuse to listen and storm off without sorting
      things out . . . etc.

– Decide how you will behave during the meeting: e.g. calmly, sympathetically, gently, to the point, honestly...

– Decide upon a compromise you would be happy to settle for if your desired outcome becomes impossible to achieve.

Step four: Being assertive during the confrontation

– Remember your rights and needs are as important as everybody else's.

– Speak clearly.

– Outline specifically and concisely:

      a) what the problem is, and

      b) what you want to change. Use this as your 'stock phrase'
      and stay with it.

– Keep to the point.

– Listen to the other person, consider and acknowledge their rights, needs and responsibilities. If your desired outcome remains unchanged, be fair but persistent.

– Repeat your stock phrase until your key points have been heard and acknowledged.

– If the other person throws awkward questions/opinions at you which take you away from your point, respond by repeating your stock phrase. (You don't have to answer questions you would rather not.)

– Empathise with the other person but keep to your agenda. For example say: 'I hear what you're saying but (repeat stock phrase)'

– Disclose feelings and state your rights and needs to strengthen your case. For example say: 'I'm sorry that you're upset about this but I've been upset by ... for a while and I need ... to change.'

– Blame behaviours rather than the person. For example say: 'It upsets me when you try to control me' rather than: 'You upset me.'

– Take responsibility for your own feelings and behaviours, and don't blame others. For example say: 'I feel angry about...' rather than: 'You have made me angry.'

– Feed back honest positive feelings about the person/situation, to help you and the other person feel better. For example say: 'I really value you as a friend but (repeat stock phrase).'

– Work for a solution or compromise to leave both parties feeling good.

Dealing with negative feelings

An effective way of protecting the self from feeling badly after a confrontation of any kind, is to deal with negative feelings as and when they are experienced. If, for example, in a conflict situation, something is said which you strongly disagree with and you respond by feeling angry, rather than allowing your anger to rule your following behaviours, a positive way of dealing with it there and then, is to verbalise how you are feeling and to let the feeling go. Likewise if, for example, a friend asks a favour of you which you don't want to do, instead of saying 'yes' (and ending up feeling frustrated with yourself for doing something you don't want to do) or saying 'no' (and being left with feelings of guilt), be honest. Say: 'I feel guilty/bad for letting you down but I can't/don't want to…' and accept that you have behaved well within your rights and have nothing to feel guilty about.

Making decisions

When faced with making a decision, before responding, try getting into the habit of taking two or three seconds to ask yourself what *you want* to do. (Instant gut reaction is often a good indication.) Remember that you have the right to choose and to state a preferred option and that it is not your responsibility to choose an undesired option, for the sake of keeping everybody else happy. Once you have made a decision, state clearly what you want, stand by your decision and deal with any consequences that result by being honest and assertive. You might choose, for example, to justify your decision by stating your needs and/or to let negative feelings go by verbalising them in acknowledgement of another's resulting position. Whatever the outcome, it's often helpful to remember that if somebody else genuinely did not want to either hear or respect your choice, they wouldn't or shouldn't have bothered to ask you to make a decision in the first place.

Saying 'No'

An eight point guide to saying 'no' painlessly can be found in the diary entry for October 22nd, 1990.

Asking for needs to be met

As above, a guide for learning how to ask for needs to be met can be found in the diary entry for October 24th, 1990.

Self-Awareness Exercises

Identifying needs/wants/would likes/dreams/aspirations etc.

For each of the following statements write down:
- Ten things I would like…
- Ten things I need…
- Ten things I enjoy doing…
- Ten things I would love to find time to do…
- Ten things I would love to achieve in my lifetime…
- Ten wishes I would love to come true…

If at first this seems a little difficult to do, just jot down what you can for the time being and try adding to the lists as and when other things come to you.

Identifying thoughts and feelings

Write down as many emotions as you can think of (positive and negative) and as above, try and identify ten things that cause you to feel each emotion.

Try asking yourself questions that you have never asked yourself before. You might choose, for example, to ask yourself what it is that *really* scares you, or how you *really* think other people view you, and so on. An excellent question to help you understand why you've developed an eating disorder, might quite simply be: 'Why do I need my anorexia/bulimia, what purpose is it serving?'

Identifying personal behaviours to be changed in order to become more effective

On a blank piece of paper write the following headings and beneath each, list those behaviours and parts of your life you would like to work on, for example:

How I see myself and my life now	How I would like myself and my life to be
– unhappy	– happier, fun and sometimes exciting
– always rushed	– more organised, on time more often
– unable to ask for help	– able to ask for help when I need it
– stupid	– able to make mistakes without feeling bad
– with no time for myself	– able to have space and time to do what I want sometimes

Creating direction – identifying life boundaries and setting goals

Identifying life boundaries

List those areas of your life you would like to enjoy more or be more in control of.

For example:

time	career	feeling happy with myself
space	fun	being impulsive
relationships	needs	dreams, aims for the future
wants	satisfaction	enjoyable things
excitement	security	

Setting goals

Taking each life boundary separately, brainstorm any ideas (as serious or as crazy as you like) you might work towards putting into practise, now or in the future, to improve or develop each.

e.g.

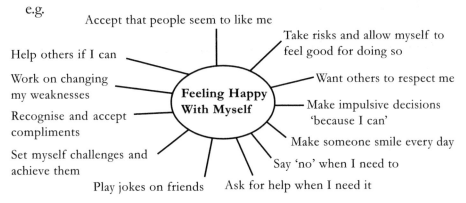

209

Once you have identified behaviours you would like to change or develop, think of each one as an individual aim and beginning with those which you perceive to be the least risky and perhaps easiest to achieve, start looking for strategies or help available to you to assist and to support you in helping yourself to begin making the changes you want.

Appendix 1

Diagnostic criteria for clinical definition of anorexia nervosa

A. Refusal to maintain body weight at or above a minimally normal weight for age and height. e.g. weight loss leading to body weight less than 85 per cent of expected OR failure to make weight gain during growth therefore leading to body weight less than 85 per cent of expected.

B. Intense fear of increased weight *or* becoming fat, even though underweight.

C. Disturbance in the way body weight or shape is experienced; Undue influence of body weight or body shape on self-evaluation; Denial of seriousness of low body weight.

D. Amenorrhoea (loss of periods for at least three months) in post-menarcheal females.

Restricting type: Does not regularly binge eat or purge.

Binge eating purging type: Regularly binge eats and purges, i.e. induces vomiting; abuses laxatives, diuretics or other medications.

Diagnostic criteria for clinical definition of bulimia nervosa

A. Recurrent episodes of binge eating. Binge eating is characterised by: i) eating large amounts of food in any two-hour period. ii) lack of control over eating during episode.

B. Recurrent inappropriate compensatory behaviour to prevent weight gain. e.g. self-induced vomiting; abusing laxatives, diuretics and enemas; fasting and excessive exercise.

C. Binge eating and inappropriate compensatory behaviour both occur at least twice a week for three months.

D. Self-evaluation is unduly influenced by body shape and weight.

E. Disturbance does not occur exclusively during episodes of anorexia nervosa.

Purging type: Regularly engages in self-induced vomiting or abuse of medication, e.g. laxatives, diuretics and enemas.

Non purging type: Does not engage in above inappropriate compensatory behaviour but does use other inappropriate compensatory behaviour such as fasting or excessive exercise.

Appendix 2

Evidence to prove that you don't need to have symptoms of 'worst-case' severity in order to have eating difficulties recognised and treated

Regardless of whether you consider your eating difficulties to be serious or not, if you are experiencing distress as a result of your eating, you are as entitled as the next person to receive medical help if you require it. With growing awareness of the distress that all eating disorders generate, doctors now recognise the need to treat all eating disorders seriously. In order to diagnose eating disorders which do not fit simply into the categories of anorexia or bulimia, The American Psychiatric Association have produced the following diagnostic criteria for recognising variation disorders.

Eating disorders not otherwise specified

The eating disorders not otherwise specified category is for disorders of eating that do not meet the criteria for any specific eating disorder. Examples include:

A. Where all criteria for anorexia nervosa are met except the female has regular menses.

B. All criteria for anorexia nervosa are met except that despite significant weight loss current weight is in normal range.

C. All criteria for bulimia nervosa are met except that binge eating and inappropriate compensatory behaviours occur less than twice a week or for a duration of less than three months.

D. Regular use of inappropriate compensatory behaviours (by individuals of normal body weight) after eating small amounts of food. e.g. self-induced vomiting after eating two cookies.

E. Repeatedly chewing and spitting out (but not swallowing) large amounts of food.

F. Binge eating disorder (BED): Recurrent episodes of binge eating in the absence of the regular use of inappropriate compensatory behaviours characteristic of bulimia nervosa.

Index

anti-depressants 59-62

assertiveness
answer to difficulties 184
behaviour options 178
compliments, giving/receiving 116
conflict, healthy handling 184
definition of 124,125, 201
equality, feelings of 103
key to recovery from anorexia 125
needs, asking to be met 131-133
needs, healthy thinking 199
needs, identifying 82, 83, 208
prevention of eating disorders 193, 194
progress 142, 143, 180, 181
recovery from eating disorders192-194
responsibilities, healthy thinking 199, 200
responsibility to meet needs 103
rights charter 198
rights, healthy thinking 198
right to have needs met 102
saying 'no' 127-130
skills I lacked 124
assertiveness, lack of/ineffectiveness 74, 103
anger, major cause of 124
anger, inability to handle 119-122
anorexia, cause of 125, 193, 194
avoiding issues 29, 92, 138, 139
conflict, inability to handle 138, 139, 177
effects of 75-80
feeling a fraud 43,44
indecisiveness 75, 103
low self-esteem 75, root of 125, 194
needs, inability to meet needs 131
needs, neglected/negated 83, 92, 125
passivity 75, 85, 92, 177, 182
passivity, low self-esteem 75

philosophy 97-99
preparing to leave 184, 185
 progress 142, 143, 180, 181 (see also **life skills**)
refusal to go 59, 65
setbacks 130, 131, 134-137, 144, 165-166
turning point 114

Eating Disorders Association 197

exercise addiction 38, 88-90

food diary 60, 64, 66-68

ineffectiveness (see **assertiveness, lack of**)

laxatives 60, 69
addiction 135-137, 140, 141, 144-147
not aiding weight loss 195
laxative withdrawal 161-173
accepting weight gain 172, 173
actual effects 161-166
avoiding issues 167, 168
dissociation 163, 166
fear of gaining weight 153, 154
fear of giving up laxatives 144-147
self-harm 165, 166
theoretical effects 149-151
ultimatum 167
weekend without laxatives 140-144
 weight gain 165

life skills/making progress
acknowledging care 155-157
asking for help 155
asking for needs to be met 131-133
challenging rejection 110-112